THE TABLES TURNED,

or

NUPKINS AWAKENED

THE TABLES TURNED,

or

NUPKINS AWAKENED

A Socialist Interlude by

WILLIAM MORRIS

Edited and with an introduction by
Pamela Bracken Wiens

OHIO UNIVERSITY PRESS

Athens

Ohio University Press, Athens, Ohio 45701
Introduction © 1994 by Pamela Bracken Wiens
Printed in the United States of America
All rights reserved

98 97 96 95 94   5 4 3 2 1

This book has been published with the support of the William Morris Society.

Library of Congress Cataloging-in-Publication Data

Morris, William, 1834–1896.
    The tables turned, or, Nupkins awakened : a socialist interlude /
by William Morris ; edited and with an introduction by Pamela
Bracken Wiens.
        p.   cm.
    Includes bibliographical references.
    ISBN 0–8214–1076–8
    1. Socialism—Drama.   I. Wiens, Pamela Bracken.   II. Title.
III. Title: Tables turned.   IV. Title: Nupkins awakened.
PR5080.T33   1994
822'.8—dc20   93–49510
                                                CIP

CONTENTS

Photograph #1: Morris at the time of the production of *The Tables Turned. William Morris Gallery, Walthamstow, London*

INTRODUCTION

illiam Morris's most active years in the early British socialist movement were accompanied by a series of unusual writing projects. From 1883 until his death in 1896, the artist-craftsman-poet who had made his fame as the "idle singer of an empty day" engaged himself in the exhaustingly active task of educating the would-be and the already-converted mass of humanity toward socialism. It was a task that George Bernard Shaw later claimed "called on [Morris's] mental reserves for the first time" and one that also called for an impressive repertoire of generic variety.

All for the cause, Morris wrote socialist chants, eulogies, lectures, essays, dialogues, book reviews, romances, histories, and—in the fall of 1887—a play. After his "little interlude," as he referred to it, was first presented on 15 October 1887, the front page of *The Pall Mall Gazette* proclaimed that Mr. William Morris, "not content with writing the songs of Socialism, . . . aspires to write its plays" (17 October 1887, 1).

Most modern readers will undoubtedly regard *The Tables Turned: or, Nupkins Awakened* as an intriguing digression in Morris's literary career. Those more familiar with the languid, narrative poetry of *The Earthly Paradise,* or with the chaotically dreamy and nightmarish quality of his now more popular *Defence of Guenevere*—or even with the archaic "Saxonisms" of the late prose romances—will find *The Tables Turned* an unusual piece indeed, a courtroom farce piled up with the kind of political and contemporary allusion of America's *Saturday Night Live* or Britain's *Monty Python.*

Few among Morris's current reading public have had access to the witty, conversational, and even "unliterary" prose found in his "little interlude" of 1887. The play was not canonized in May Morris's edition of the *Collected Works* (24 volumes, London, 1910–1915). An early, handwritten draft can be found in the Morris Collection of the Huntington Library (HM 6433) and is also now available in limited access on microfilm through Research Publications. First edition texts of the play, printed at the Socialist League's *Commonweal* newspaper offices shortly after the play's inaugural performance, are now collectors' items, the relatively few surviving copies scattered among rare book libraries and private collections in both the United Kingdom and the United States. Heretofore, the only wider public access has been through the text included in May Morris's limited print edition *William Morris: Artist, Writer, Socialist* (1936, 1966).

This textual unavailability can only have contributed to the fact that critics, even Victorianists and Morrisians, have paid little attention to *The Tables Turned*. With the exception of a few recent discussions of the play (Stetz 1990, Sargent 1990, and Wiens 1991), Morris's genuine experiment in dramatic form has been relegated to the marginal status of a biographical footnote. Although all major biographers since J. W. Mackail have mentioned the play, few have offered more than a sentence or scant page of reference to its possible significance in the fledgling development of a truly "socialist drama."

This relative silence on the subject of Morris's "socialist interlude" may in fact rest largely on an opinion established quite early in its prospective critical history, one formed by no less important a figure than Mackail, Morris's first biographer. Mackail claimed quite categorically that "as a matter of fact, nothing came of the experiment in which the method of the Towneley Mysteries was applied to a modern farce" (Mackail 1899, 2: 187). Although recognizing the influence of the cycle of medieval mystery plays Morris admired, and the contemporary plays he did not, Mackail regarded *The Tables Turned* as little more than a short detour of dramatic interest which ultimately proved to be a dead-end.

Not many contemporaries held the same view, however. The young poet W. B. Yeats insisted, for example, that Morris intended to write other plays, and that during the winter of 1888, he was in fact "writing another—of the middle ages this time" (letter to Katharine Tynan, 20 June 1888, Kelly 1986, 1: 60). No evidence of such a project has yet been uncovered, but its very mention attests to Morris's excitement about the possibilities of his dramatic

3

experiment. Almost ten years later George Bernard Shaw also recalled:

> Morris was so interested by his experiment in this sort of composition that he for some time talked of trying his hand at a serious drama, and would no doubt have done it had there been any practical occasion for it, or any means of consummating it by stage representation under proper conditions without spending more time on the job than it was worth . . . It was impossible for such a born teller and devourer of stories as he was to be indifferent to an art which is nothing more than the most vivid and real of all ways of story-telling. No man would more willingly have seen his figures move and heard their voices than he (Shaw 1932, 2: 213).

One of the most important reasons why Morris may not have rekindled his dramatic inclinations can be found in the term "proper conditions." Although the generation of young, aspiring—or soon to be aspiring—playwrights surrounding him were already contemplating the "rebirth" of drama and its political repercussions, Morris seemed to share with his older, Victorian contemporaries an antitheatrical prejudice. This prejudice was later seasoned by his view of the arts in relationship to a truly revolutionary form of socialism. Morris openly expressed dislike for what Shaw referred to as "the contemporary theatrical routine of the Strand" (Shaw 1932, 2: 210), and he had severe doubts that proper dramatic conditions could exist until "after the Change." Morris once wrote,

> Now-a-days the arts have fallen into such a miserable state of degradation . . . [and] as to the stage itself,

4

it seems to me that of all the arts the drama, acting in all its forms, has sunk the lowest . . . How can it be otherwise? Society is rotten to the core and only waits for revolution to sweep it away: in the new society only lies the hope for the Arts. (letter to James Frederick Henderson, 28 December 1885, Kelvin, 1884, 1987, 2: 507–08)

As he was to later elaborate in his collaborative vision of Socialism, titled *Socialism: Its Growth and Outcome,* he believed that the drama as "a wholly co-operative art . . . could be more easily and pleasantly dealt with by a communal society working co-operatively" (Morris and Bax 1893, 311).

In the light of his aversion to almost all aspects of "the routine of the Strand," as well as the absence of those revolutionary conditions allowing a co-operative art, it may seem surprising that Morris would indeed have complied with what Shaw remembered as a request to provide "a dramatic entertainment" to "raise the wind" of the Socialist League (Shaw 1932, 2: 211). Dramatic entertainments had become regular features of League and other socialist organizations' entertainment repertoires, though evidence from the advertisements of socialist newspapers of the day, such as *The Commonweal,* suggests that most of these had been short dramatic pieces or one-act plays appropriated from the texts of popular East and West End theatre playwrights. As Raphael Samuel, Ewan MacColl, and Stuart Cosgrove note in their seminal work, *Theatres of the Left,* these plays were primarily regarded as "adjunct forms of entertainment" (12) and not as ideological reinforcement or propaganda.

5

Morris's "little interlude" appears to mark an important shift in this appropriation practice. An early *Commonweal* advertisement for *The Tables Turned* includes the important pronouncement "ON SATURDAY OCTOBER 15 . . . AN ORIGINAL DRAMATIC SKETCH WILL BE PRODUCED FOR THE FIRST TIME" (1 October 1887, 320). Within the next few years other "original" plays were produced for League entertainments, now written by fellow League members no doubt influenced by Morris's interlude.

The co-operative and communal spirit of such amateur productions, written "by and for the people," seems to have struck Morris with a spiritual sense of the medieval guild play. This may have fueled the energy he expressly put to work on what he self-consciously referred to (perhaps for the first time in a letter to Georgiana Burne-Jones dated 24 September) as an interlude: "I have been writing a—what?—an 'interlude' let's call it, to be acted at Farringdon Road for the benefit of Commonweal" (Kelvin 1984, 1987, 2: 695).

This seemingly arbitrary label suggests Morris's spiritual allegiance to medieval dramatic traditions. By the mid-nineteenth century, the theatrical connotation of the term "interlude" included "popular stage plays or comedies" (OED), but Morris—with his great affection for and knowledge of the Middle Ages—may have been applying interlude in the sense of the light, humorous pieces "commonly introduced between the acts of the long mystery-plays or moralities" (OED).

Morris's sense of the comic in drama was naturally inclined toward the humor of the medieval playwright. Shaw remembered, for example, Morris quoting "with great relish . . . scenes in the Towneley Mysteries between the 'shepherds abiding in the field'" and claiming them as "his idea of a good bit of comedy" (Shaw 1932, 2: 210). Not surprisingly, Morris's general dislike of the Renaissance extended to an indictment of the "absurd" set of dramatic conventions that had begun with Shakespeare (Kelvin 1984, 1987, 2: 507). May Morris later remarked that her father believed "Shakespeare had done great harm to the drama . . . having imposed a certain tradition on the future, which no one after him has been strong enough to get away from" (May Morris 1910–15, 22: xxvii).

The interlude label therefore seemed appropriate, and when the play was later printed by the offices of *Commonweal,* Morris subtitled it, "A Socialist Interlude."

The production of Morris's interlude did proceed in the spiritual vein of a medieval guild play. Like its medieval prototype, the entire production of *The Tables Turned* affirmed the camaraderie of a group of "fellows," being written and performed by members of a fellowship of "co-workers" in the cause. The printed text of the play includes in its list of "Dramatis Personae" the original members of the cast, all of whom were active members in the Socialist League.

Even the content of *The Tables Turned* reveals its undeniably subtle link to the rough and boisterous comedy of his beloved Towneley mysteries. As one biographer notes, Morris's play was a "queer" production, "a kind of collaborative effort by a pageant-master with a bluff sense of humour, and the Evangelist John" (Bloomfield 1934, 259).

7

Indeed, like his Wakefield master, Morris combined contemporary allusion with comedy, broad farce, and, in his case, the religion of socialism. As in *The Second Shepherd's Play,* Morris ultimately balanced an optimistic ending with social complaint. Although Nupkins, like Mak, fears the death penalty from a people's court, he ultimately receives only comic retribution for his sins. At the end of Morris's interlude, however, socialists—not shepherds—sing together in harmony.

Despite Morris's proclivity for the medieval, however, an irony of *The Tables Turned* is its surprising link to many features of the popular Victorian stage play, that is, to the farce and melodrama of the very Strand to which he admitted a strong aversion. Morris adapted several classic melodramatic elements: the confrontation of good versus evil, the false accusation, the final denouement into poetic justice, and the use of musical accompaniment. The opening courtroom scene of the play was in fact a common one in many East End melodramas. But the farcical elements in the play are more readily apparent and include the kind of slapstick antics demonstrated by the inept court clerk in Part I.

Morris also peopled his interlude with the kind of typecast characters standard in both popular dramatic forms. Characters with such evocative names as Mary Pinch and Jack Freeman are like the innocent and falsely accused victims of melodrama. Mary's personal testimony reveals that her whole life is lived in a "pinch," a slang term which provided a double edge of humour, as it connoted both stealing (the accusation against poor Mary) and "to bring into difficulties or troubles, to afflict or harass'' (OED). One of the villains in the piece is none other than the lawyer, Mr. Hungary, who almost lives up to the melodramatic stereotype of the shifty and dishonest lawyer. (Grimsted 1968, 201). He is "hungry" for anything but justice, and has an appetite instead for "making Socialists pay." Hungary's testimony against Pinch and Freeman, the "hero" of Part I—who continues to conduct himself, though accused, as a "free man"—is provided by bumbling and perjuring policemen with the equally evocative names Sergeant Sticktoit and Constable Stongithoath.

Morris's professed preference for simplicity of characterization and his aversion for "elaborate realism" on the stage (May Morris 1910–15, 22: xxvii) actually aligns itself to both early and late dramatic traditions, to medieval drama's one dimensional "vice" and "virtue" characters and to nineteenth-century farce and melodrama's equally evocative—and pedagogic—dramatis personae. In his adaptation of simple iconographical symbols for many of his characters, Morris was aligning himself to important conventions of both forms. Shaw in fact noted this propensity, declaring that Morris "always contended that no more was necessary for stage illusion than some distinct conventional symbol, such as a halo for a saint, a crook for a bishop, or if you like, a cloak and dagger for the villain, and a red wig for the comedian" (Shaw 1932, 2: 212). And when Morris created his own Archbishop of Canterbury, he identified him by such symbols as "a pair of clerical bands and black stockings" (213).

An unusual hybrid of medieval and contemporary stage

conventions, Morris's "little interlude" would prove to be
something new to its audience. Its enthusiastic *Gazette* reviewer went so far as to consider it a regenerated alterna-
tive to already existing dramatic forms.

> [The] two or three hundred people who crowded the
> hall of the Socialist League on Saturday night assisted,
> perhaps, at the birth, or at any rate the regeneration,
> of a dramatic form destined to supplant the milk-and-
> water comedies and 'leggy' burlesques in which our
> bloated capitalism delights. (*Pall Mall Gazette* 17 Octo-
> ber 1887, 1)

The final product of Morris's eclectic dramatic compo-
sition was, all records seem to agree, an exhausting and yet
energizing piece of amateurish collaboration. Despite what
proved to be the light and comic vein of the interlude,
once Morris had accepted the task he went to work on it
with typical gusto. Almost a month ahead of its opening
performance, he claimed to be "still very busy about interlude" in a letter to May (Kelvin 1984, 1987, 2: 694). His
energies resulted in the creation of an artfully balanced
dramatic structure with two "trial" scenes (or "Parts" as
the earliest printed text indicates) ironically mirroring one
another. The bourgeois courtroom of Justice Nupkins in
Part I of the interlude is thereby reversed and comically
corrected in the outdoor, folk-mootish Council of the
Commune in Part II.

Morris's choice of the courtroom scene for Part I seems
quite appropriate. His involvement in several important legal infractions on the issue of free speech is well docu-
mented in both his Socialist Diary and in his daughter's

A SCENE FROM MR. WILLIAM MORRIS'S SOCIALISTIC PLAY

THE TABLES TURNED; OR, NUPKINS AWAKENED.

Photograph #4: A sketch of the first act of the opening performance of *The Tables Turned,* which appeared on the front page of *The Pall Mall Budget,* 3 November 1887. *New York State Library, Special Collections*

accounts of his socialist activities in *William Morris: Artist, Writer, Socialist.* Earlier in 1887, Morris had recorded his disgust with the Norwich affair, a demonstration of unemployed workers which led to some window smashing and a sentence of nine months for one of its leaders. Morris particularly noted his disdain for the judge, whose "summing up of the case was amusing and instructive . . . showing a sort of survival of the old sort of bullying . . . mixed with a grotesque attempt at modernization on philanthropic lines; it put me in a great rage" (25 January 1887 in Boos 1981, 20). Again on 23 February, Morris marked his disapproval of both the steep fines involved in a magistrate's punishment of a poor Leaguer arrested for street preaching and of the rough treatment of poor East Enders by the police (Boos 1981, 34).

May also elaborated on her father's involvement in the kind of "Free Speech in London" confrontations which Part I of the play recounts. These had begun as early as 1885. She quotes his outrage against both the courts and the police:

> On May 17 [1885] . . . occurred the first of the series of Police outrages which we have had to endure . . . The Socialist League took an active part in the attempt to vindicate before the Courts the freedom of citizens, which was of course unsuccessful. (May Morris 1936, 1: 223)

One of these courtroom confrontations involved Morris directly. As the treasurer of the League's Committee of Defense, Morris either stood bail or helped defend League members arrested for any infringements on the right to assemble and make public demonstration. In September of 1885, this role led to a somewhat comical court proceeding during which Morris was himself arrested for having called out "Shame" and hissing after the judge had passed a sentence of two months' hard labor on the defendant. In a fashion that now seems quite appropriate to the way her father would later make dramatic use of the incident in *The Tables Turned,* May described her father's day in court as a theatrical production.

> The various accounts of the next day's proceedings . . . read like a scene in a comic opera. Picture the

Thames Police-court on an autumn morning, the actors, a magistrate of limited vision and no sense of humour, angry policeman ready to lie through thick and thin, in the dock a poor East-end Jew tailor, who is convicted for—apparently accidentally—kicking a policeman; later steps up a world-renowned poet charged with disturbance in court, and after a humorous dialogue with the magistrate, let off because he **was** famous; chorus and crowd made up of the police rushing everyone around . . . and the London sightseers only too happy over any sort of public shindy. (May Morris 1936, 1: 225)

Morris obviously had first-hand and ready fuel for a biting satirical look at unfair judges and inept policeman. But he also seemed intent upon satirizing the bourgeois establishment that supported such a system of justice. Ironically the three witnesses for the defendant, Jack Freeman, are none other than the Archbishop of Canterbury, Alfred Lord Tennyson (another "world-renowned poet"), and the famous scientist, John Tyndall. Morris's opinion of these famous Victorian leaders and their utter lack of understanding for the socialist movement was used to effectively comic ends.

Morris's correspondence in September of 1887 suggests that he was not just concerned with writing a play as the mouthpiece for his frustrations with the free speech in London confrontations, however. In fact, he ended up demonstrating an appreciable interest in a well-rounded sphere of theatrical production, engaging himself not only as writer and actor, but as active director and producer as well. As

The Tables Turned's producer, he carefully designated appropriate actors to specific parts. On 21 September he wrote May, "I was obliged to nail Miss Courthorne for the woman's part, not being sure of you for rehearsals . . . I have got it all roughed in now, and the reading is to come off after this day or two. I feel very shy about it I must say" (Kelvin 1984, 1987, 2: 692).

The same letter indicates that Shaw, already with some amount of amateur stage experience, had consented to take the role of the Archbishop of Canterbury. Later it appears that Shaw had to decline the role, and Morris then asked Walter Crane, his artist friend and also a League member, to read the part (Crane 1907, 261). At last resort however, Morris himself had to play the prelate, which may account for H. A. Barker's later memories of opening night for the *Walthamstow Weekly Times and Echo*. He recalled that Morris as "[h]is Grace of Canterbury," like the other cast members packed into the wings of the small stage, was, "with the rest, in a high state of excitement . . . due, in part probably, to the fact that this was his first appearance as actor and dramatist." Morris, trying to stay aware of everything that was going on, "got excited again," forgot his own part and had to improvise his lines (from *Walthamstow Weekly* 15 November 1896, cited in Thompson 1976, 699).

Shaw was nonetheless impressed with the final and overall effect of Morris's performance. Ten years later, he also recalled for his *Saturday Review* readers: "Morris played the ideal Archbishop. He made no attempt to make up the part in the ordinary stage fashion . . . [this] he did by obliterating his humor and intelligence, and presenting his own person to the audience like a lantern with the light blown out, with a dull absorption in his own dignity which several minutes of the wildest screaming laughter at him when he entered could not disturb'' (Shaw 1932, 2: 212–13).

This stylized role-playing on the part of Morris appears to have been intended with no personal malice toward the current Archbishop of Canterbury, Edward White Benson, a prelate whom Morris knew through the Firm's work in ecclesiastical design (Kelvin 1984, 1987, 1: 521). In his own ''realization'' of character, Morris dispensed with straight parody or, as the *Pall Mall Gazette* review indicates, impersonation:

> In a shovel hat and with large white bands Mr. Morris looked more like an Archmandrite than an archbishop, and his beard, of course, put out of the question any attempt to ''make up'' in imitation of Mr. Benson. (17 October 1887, 1)

The shorter role of defense witness John Tyndall, leading Victorian scientist and friend of T. H. Huxley, was equally free of direct character representation, though Morris would surely have used him as a type of bourgeois single-mindedness. For this role he chose H. Bartlett, a ''young gentleman,'' the anonymous reviewer noted, ''if possible still more unlike his prototype'' (*Pall Mall Gazette,* 17 October 1887, 1).

For the part of Tennyson, however, Morris was willing to play up the parody of a fellow poet—or at least to allow the actor to play full reign with it. Shaw recalled that for this role, Morris carefully chose a socialist (a Mr. A. Brookes)

15

"who happened to combine the right sort of beard with a melancholy temperament, and drilled him in a certain portentous incivility of speech which, taken with the quality of his remarks, threw a light on Morris's opinion of Tennyson which was all the more instructive because he delighted in Tennyson's verse" (Shaw 1932, 2: 212). The *Gazette* reviewer also noted that "the representative of Lord Tennyson . . . with his bald head, his long beard, and his flowing Inverness cloak, vaguely suggested the Laureate, whose manner, too, he was popularly reported to reproduce" (1). When Brooke's Tennyson recited his scripted line, "I don't want to understand Socialism: it doesn't belong to my time," both his contemporary audience—and the modern reader—can recognize Morris's own quibble with the venerable Laureate's ostrich-like response to the relevance of the socialist movement.

As an active director, Morris's attention to the details of casting seemed to be matched by his perfectionism in regard to the production. More than thirty years later another cast member, John Turner, then a union activist, recalled the rehearsals. Though playing only a minor role, that of the inept court clerk, "he remembered more than anything else the strong language used by the producer at the rehearsals and how fiercely Morris stamped and shouted when things went wrong" (Arnot 1964, 87).

The opening night of Morris's "coming out as a playwright" was accompanied by a certain amount of fanfare, deserving no doubt of Morris's wider literary reputation. Shaw noted that one dramatic critic "took care to be present—Mr. William Archer" (Shaw 1932, 2: 213). We may assume that either Archer, or Shaw himself—who was at this time a professional dramatic critic—wrote the *Gazette*'s front page review of the play. It appeared the following Monday, October 17, under the bold headline, "ARISTO-PHANES IN FARRINGDON ROAD: A Socialist Interlude by the Author of 'THE EARTHLY PARADISE'." The anonymous reviewer dramatically recounted the ambiance of the scene:

> The hall of the Socialist League is, in fact, a long, nar-row garret, with whitewashed roof and rafters, and red-ochred walls, boasting as their sole decoration a photograph of Karl Marx . . . and a few red flags which look as if they had 'braved a thousand years the bobbies and the breeze.' The whole available width of stage is certainly not more than fifteen feet, with a depth of perhaps eight or ten—a rather narrow cradle for a new art form. The audience was mainly com-posed of the working-class Socialists, who naturally form the bulk of the League, but there was also a sprinkling of artistic Utopians. (*Pall Mall Gazette,* 17 October 1887, 1)

Among this sprinkling were such notable artistic and lit-erary figures as Walter Crane, who later referred to it as "a very interesting performance" (Crane 1907, 261), and Yeats's young friend Ernest Rhys. Over forty years later, Rhys recounted the dramatic moment right before the play's opening, when Jane Burden Morris swept in:

17

> before the curtain went up, I had the sensation of see-ing a figure, which might have stepped straight out of a pre-Raphaelite picture, passing through the audience.

It was Mrs. Morris, whose superb tall form, long neck, and austere, handsome pale features looked more queenly than any Guinevere or Cleopatra. (Rhys 1931, 53)

According to the *Commonweal* review, the drawing of the curtain revealed "a very effective . . . and realistic" court scene designed by the stage manager, H. A. Barker, and his wife. This was replaced in scene two—described in the stage directions as "The Fields near a Country Village; a Copse close by"—with a "pretty Landscape, with its tree for the open-air communal council, and its dwellings in the distance" designed by a "Mr. Campfield" (*Commonweal,* 5 November 1887, 350).

Although the opening night performance was beset with a few of the mishaps of any amateur theatrical—not only did Morris forget his lines, but at the climactic moment when he was making his entrance, "Lord Tennyson fainted in the wings . . . [and] the prompter struggled into his get up" (from *Walthamstow Weekly* 15 November cited in Thompson 1976, 699)—*Commonweal* proclaimed it a dramatic success. On 22 October 1887 it was reported that

The play was well received and much applauded. So many people were unable to obtain admittance that it decided to repeat the performance this Saturday (Oct. 22), when the same tickets will be available. Performances are also being arranged for Hammersmith and Bloomsbury; and it was further announced that any Radical Club or branch of the League or S.D.F. possessing a stage and willing to aid in the raising of the *Commonweal* Fund, could arrange with the manager to

Photograph 3: According to announcements in the socialist news-paper, *Commonweal,* the Coach House—meeting room of the Hammersmith Socialist League—was the location for a perfor-mance of *the Tables Turned* on 5 November 1887, and possibly again in January of 1888. With its realistic set and properties, the production at Hammersmith must have been scaled down. *William Morris Gallery, Walthamstow, London*

have the same company, scenery etc . . . (*Common-weal* 22 October 1887, 343)

At least eleven more performances were advertised in the pages of *Commonweal* between October of 1887 and June of 1888, varying in location from large halls to local clubs, like the small meeting room of the Hammersmith branch of the Socialist League where the play was billed for 5 November 1887. After the second performance at the Athenaeum Hall (22 October 1887), the anarchist Prince Kropotkin and his friend Elisée Reclus, the French geog-

Photograph #2: May Morris dressed in the kind of costume and playing the guitar as she very likely would have appeared in the musical finale of the play. *William Morris Gallery, Walthamstow, London*

rapher, were reportedly "talking of putting Nupkins into a French dress, and sending him forth to do additional good in that fashion" (*Commonweal,* 5 November 1887, 350).

One of the last performances appears to have been as late as 17 June 1888—by professional theatrical standards a healthy run for any play—when a performance at the International Club for the East-End Propaganda Fund was given by what *Commonweal* now referred to as "the Nupkins Company":

> On Sunday . . . the Nupkins Company gave a dramatic representation of "*The Tables Turned*" to a large audience who thoroughly appreciated the various points in the play. (*Commonweal* 23 June 1888, 200)

Yeats was one of the appreciative among the audience of this performance. He wrote to Katharine Tynan on 20 June 1888:

> I was at the east end of London to see Morris act in his Socialist play. He really acts very well. Miss Morris does not act at all but remains her self most charmingly throughout her part . . ." (cited in Kelly 1986, 1: 74)

Yeats's interest in the play seems to have preceded its performance. Three months earlier he had sent a copy of the play to Katharine. "I send you a copy of Morris's play," he wrote on 11 April 1888; "it is a little soiled as it is one of the copies used by the actors—no others being to be had" (cited in Kelly, 1: 59–60).

By April of 1888, *Commonweal* copies of the play were in print, but perhaps because of the relatively small print runs made in their printing offices, copies may have been hard to find due to the play's already healthy reading audience. For four shillings, the curious as well as the unconverted could read the fruits of Morris's coming out as a playwright.

The propaganda potential of an original production such as *The Tables Turned* was immediately recognized by its *Commonweal* reviewers. Although stage historians Ralph Samuel, Ewan MacColl, and Stuart Cosgrove point out that agit-prop, or self-consciously political propaganda theater, was not formally developed in those early days of socialism, the possibilities for theatrical conversions were obviously recognized by the "Nupkins' Company." A *Commonweal* review dated 5 November 1887 clearly stated that two subsequent performances were well attended, and that the audiences included "many people who are not often seen at a Socialist meeting; and in this way there is no doubt that some good propagandistic work is being done" (350).

Part I of the play undoubtedly functioned cathartically for the League members in the audiences, offering comedy in the most generally accepted theoretical sense of "the baring of teeth to the enemy" (Barreca 1988, 8). But Part II of *The Tables Turned* was indeed much more, for it allowed Morris the opportunity to fulfill his own demand for art to show people "things decidedly above their daily life" (Kelvin 1984, 1987, 2: 36). Though his dramatic techniques were far from the more "sophisticated" theoretical advancements of later agit-prop and particularly workerist theater, Morris's play was nonetheless an obvious attempt at drama for the purpose of propaganda. In its revolutionary artfulness, an equation Samuel, MacColl, and Cosgrove them-

22

selves claim as constitutive of agit-prop (xix), *The Tables Turned* was left-wing drama providing more than entertainment and demonstrating—unlike many other plays of the period—politically engaged, rather than merely socially conscious performance (Samuel, MacColl, and Cosgrove 1985, xviii).

One Morris biographer has recognized Morris's socialist interlude as breaking "new ground in the creation of agit prop" (Lindsay, 1975, 324). Though later agit-prop would turn to visions of the future, Morris's "new ground" was of a decidedly nostalgic nature and turned perhaps inevitably toward models from his own beloved Middle Ages and its equally polemic morality plays. This medievalesque "simplicity" Morris advocated as a virtue in all of the arts, including the drama, and it was very likely the source of inspiration for socialist plays for the next few decades.

Twenty years later, for example, a short play titled *Brotherhood* was widely staged in an adjunct variety of socialist society, the Socialist Sunday School. In its pedagogic echo of *The Tables Turned* it offered its young initiates a vision of ideal characters to imitate and ultimately celebrated a socialist victory of virtue over vice. Like Morris's play, *Brotherhood* begins with a courtroom scene in which "the Working Man has been convicted for stealing." The climax of the play also incorporates a scene in which a socialist comrade interrupts a policeman's attempt to take away the convicted prisoner. The final scene of *Brotherhood*, like that of *The Tables Turned,* concludes in a beatified post-revolutionary vision in which "all [are] singing in beautiful chorus" (Samuel, MacColl, and Cosgrove 1985, 15).

23

Despite its obvious influence on later socialist drama, the play has drawn sporadic criticism. Some have faulted *The Tables Turned* for its blatant, unabashed idealism (no doubt a reference to Part II) and for its bourgeois, even counterproductive use of humour.

Not all of Morris's literary and artistic contemporaries offered effusive praise for his dramatic and visionary experimentation. William Holman Hunt, the Pre-Raphaelite painter, joined others of Morris's circle in criticizing his socialism. While he strongly praised Morris as an artist and poet, Hunt found Morris's political views to be misguided. For him *The Tables Turned* proved this view. Hunt once advised a friend to read "Nupkins Awakened" as a good example of Morris's political and ideological naivete (Edith Hunt typescript of Hunt letter to an anonymous recipient, Item 42, Kenneth Spencer Research Library, University of Kansas).

However, judged by purely aesthetic, or even dramatic standards, Morris's vision of an idyllic, agrarian, post-revolutionary society achieved without bloodshed and maintained without malice or a need for revenge is consistent with his philosophy of art. May Morris explained that her father believed "[n]obody should be killed on the stage, of course, and no sick or dying persons should be presented" (May Morris 1910–15, 22: xxvii). And Morris himself once wrote that "those who want to make art educational must accept the necessity of showing people things decidedly above their daily life" (Letter to Thomas Coglan Horsfall, 24 March 1881, Kelvin 1984, 1987, 2: 36).

Later criticism of *The Tables Turned* follows in a some-

24

what similar vein. Recently, in one of the few discussions of the play to emerge in post-modern critical discussion, Margaret Stetz expressed severe skepticism about the value of Morris's bourgeois sense of comedy, especially in regard to anarchism. She claims that Morris's complicity in "the fin-de-siecle comic discourse about anarchism" helped "to check the spread of that philosophy in England" (Stetz 1990, 3). But if Morris's "peculiar attempt at political high comedy" (3) did indeed succeed in turning the tables on anarchism as Stetz contends, it was one of his own problematic intentions. Morris's relationship to anarchism, and more particularly to the divisive faction of anarchists within the Socialist League itself, was at one point quite clear. Despite his friendship with the anarchist, Prince Kropotkin, Morris stood firmly against their philosophy and noted that "[t]he Anarchist element in us seem determined to drive things to extremity and break us up if we do not declare for Anarchy: which I for one will not do" (letter to Bruce Glasier, Kelvin 1984, 1987, 2: 841).

The Tables Turned does not satirize only the anarchist faction of the Socialist League, however. Morris's satire is leveled at all of the divisions within the current body of British socialism. The play is full of insider jokes and topical allusions to not only the Anarchists, and their familiarity with "the use of dynamite," but to members of the Social Democratic Federation, described by Lawyer Hungary in the play as one of two "dangerous and malevolent associations," and to the Fabians, labeled again by Hungary as "the third and most dangerous" of all "three principle societies." After comically rechristening them, Morris could

25

poke fun at the eccentric personal practices of some well-recognized Fabians, among these Shaw's avid vegetarianism, Annie Besant's conversion to theosophy, and Sydney Webb's rigidly mechanical economic theory.

Above all, the humour and satire in *The Tables Turned* does not seem to have insulted the "political correctness" of any of the principle socialist societies for whom it was performed. Its strongest endorsement was perhaps demonstrated by Kropotkin and Reclus's interest in taking the piece abroad.

Beyond the play's polemic posturing, however, one may make some legitimate criticisms of Morris's experimentation in theatrical prose. Despite the liveliness of several key interactions between characters in *The Tables Turned,* specific passages can be no better described than flat or wooden. Mary Pinch's long soliloquy-like defense in Part I of the play—in which she describes at some length first the beauty and then the hardship of the country life that led her to London—though particularly expressive of Morris's empathy for the plight of the transplanted London laborer, is perhaps the best example of a prose style not quite suited to stage performance. Readers will note its Nowhereian flavor, but most will, in any case, puzzle over poor Mary's sophisticated diction and Morrisian expressiveness. Morris seemed better able to consistently sustain an overall conversational prose in the few dialogues he contributed to *Commonweal;* among these "Honesty is the Best Policy; or the Inconvenience of Stealing" (November 1887) and "Whigs Astray" (January 1889).

Readers of this edition will no doubt find other criticisms and/or disappointments in *The Tables Turned*. Some will conclude that the interlude is not at all what they would expect of the better known sensibilities of William Morris. The sarcastic humour, contemporary parody, and overall realistic ambiance of especially Part I seem far removed from Morris's medievalesque temper. *The Tables Turned* is far less "Morrisian" than, for example, the kind of pageant plays which circulated throughout England for the next few decades. Pageant plays—or masques as they were often called—like those produced by Walter Crane seem much more in tune with Morris's earlier proclamations in *Socialism: Its Growth and Outcome* about what makes appropriate or valuable drama. Crane's masque, *Beauty's Awakening: A Masque of Winter and Spring* (1899), for example, offers the kind of visual tableaux and ideological correctness we might expect of a Morris drama (Crane 1907, 452–455). We may speculate that Crane's masque took the shape which Morris's subsequently planned yet unwritten, or undiscovered, play of the Middle Ages might have.

Despite its previous reputation as an unlikely and uncharacteristic one-time experiment in the career of a prolific and diverse Victorian figure, *The Tables Turned* has gained a trickle of attention from avid Morrisians. At least three groups have restaged or attempted to restage the play for modern audiences. Morris's dramatic experiment can and should be regarded as an intriguing biographical commentary on his admirable and eclectic energies. But it also offers evidence of several other worthy literary and aesthetic concerns.

Immediately of interest to Morris students and scholars

27

is the play's demonstration of Morris's biting satiric ability, as well as his highly colloquial prose style, which could (at points) accommodate lively and humorous dialogue. *The Tables Turned* reveals his largely unrecognized conversational style, one which balances out his more visible reputation as the archaic poet/dreamer of an idle day. Additionally, the play will be of interest to social historians, as it offers a valuable compendium of political allusion highlighted by the sensibilities and attitudes of the socialist movement in its formative stages. And, finally, Morris's socialist interlude will be of interest to theater historians and students of early workerist theater. Morris's *The Tables Turned* is a noteworthy and commendable example of employing original works to the leftist cause before theories of agit prop and left-wing theater were developed and espoused.

Morris's socialist interlude is indeed more than an intriguing digression in his prolific and eclectic career. Unlike his first biographer, J. W. Mackail, modern readers may now be able to ascertain for themselves whether something came of "the experiment in which the method of the Towneley Mysteries was applied to a modern farce," both in terms of its contemporary "success" and possibly even in terms of its more far-reaching influence on the Socialist cause and its place in the development of dramatic art forms as the vehicle for Socialist propaganda and education. As this edition sets out to demonstrate, Morris's "little interlude" is not so little after all. *The Tables Turned; or, Nupkins Awakened* provides new ground for critical attention to yet another worthy and worthwhile Morris experiment.

28

Editor's Note: The play text is typeset from a first edition, printed in London at the office of *The Commonweal* in 1887 with the title, *The Tables Turned; Or, Nupkins Awakened. A Socialist Interlude.* In preparation of the Introduction, Notes, and manuscript, I would like to thank Mark Samuels Lasner and the William Morris Society of the United States and Peter Cormack at the William Morris Gallery in Walthamstow, London. For helping to clarify points of British social history, as well as editing an early draft of the introduction, I owe much thanks to Frank Sharp. And for his patience and support, my gratitude to Clifton.

Pamela Bracken Wiens
The Catholic University of America
Washington, D.C.

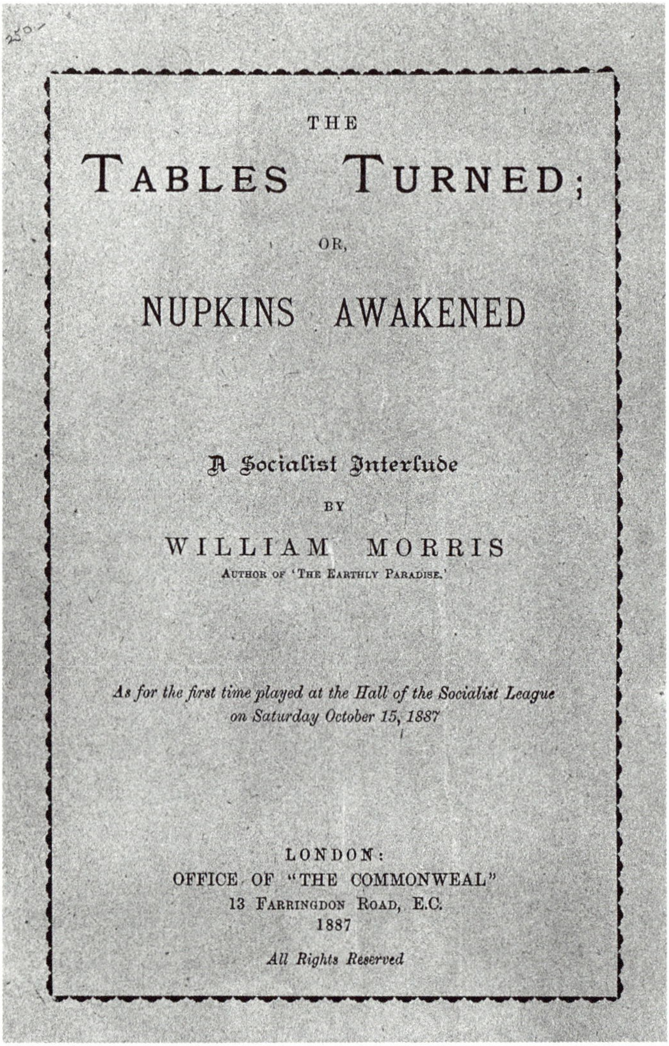
THE
TABLES TURNED;
OR,
NUPKINS AWAKENED
A Socialist Interlude
BY
WILLIAM MORRIS
AUTHOR OF 'THE EARTHLY PARADISE.'
As for the first time played at the Hall of the Socialist League
on Saturday October 15, 1887
LONDON:
OFFICE OF "THE COMMONWEAL"
13 FARRINGDON ROAD, E.C.
1887
All Rights Reserved

Photograph 5: William Morris, *The Tables Turned,* front cover. Collection of Mark Samuels Lasner.

THE TABLES TURNED,

or

NUPKINS AWAKENED

PART I.

SCENE.—*A Court of Justice.*

USHER, CLERK OF THE COURT, MR. HUNGARY, Q.C., and others. MR. LA-DI-DA, *the prisoner, not in the dock, but seated in a chair before it.*

[*Enter* MR. JUSTICE NUPKINS.[1]]

Usher. Silence!—silence!

Mr. Justice Nupkins. Prisoner at the bar, you have been found guilty by a jury, after a very long and careful consideration of your remarkable and strange case, of a very serious offence; an offence which squeamish moralists are apt to call robbing the widow and orphan; a cant phrase also, with which I hesitate to soil my lips, designates this offence as swindling. You will permit me to remark that the very fact that such nauseous and improper words can be used about the conduct of a *gentleman* shows how far you have been led astray from the path traced out for the feet of a respectable member of society. Mr. La-di-da, if you were less self-restrained, less respectful, less refined, less of a gentleman, in short, I might point out to you with

33

more or less severity the disastrous consequences of your conduct; but I cannot doubt, from the manner in which you have borne yourself during the whole of this trial, that you are fully impressed with the seriousness of the occasion. I shall say no more then, but perform the painful duty which devolves on me of passing sentence on you. I am compelled in doing so to award you a term of imprisonment; but I shall take care that you shall not be degraded by contamination with thieves and rioters, and other coarse persons, or share the diet and treatment which is no punishment to persons used to hard living: that would be to inflict a punishment on you not intended by the law, and would cast a stain on your character not easily wiped away. I wish you to return to that society of which you have up to this untoward event formed an ornament without any such stain. You will, therefore, be imprisoned as a first-class misdemeanant for the space of one calendar month; and I trust that during the retirement thus enforced upon you, which to a person of your resources should not be very irksome, you will reflect on the rashness, the incaution, the impropriety, in one word, of your conduct, and that you will never be discovered again appropriating to your personal use money which has been entrusted to your care by your friends and relatives.[2]

Mr. La-di-da. I thank you, my lord, for your kindness and consideration. May I be allowed to ask you to add to your kindness by permitting me to return to my home and make some necessary arrangements before submitting myself to the well-merited chastisement which my imprudence has brought upon me?

Mr. J. N. Certainly. I repeat I do not wish to make your sentence any heavier by forcing a hard construction upon it. I give you a week to make all arrangements necessary for your peace of mind and your bodily comfort.

Mr. L. I thank your lordship.

[*Exit.*]

[*The case of* MARY PINCH *called.*]

Mr. Hungary,[3] *Q.C.* I am for the prosecution, my lord, instructed by the Secretary of State for the Home Department. (JUDGE *bites his pen and nods.*) My lord, and gentlemen of the Jury, although this case may seem to some ill-judging persons a trivial one, I think you will be able to see before it is over that it is really important in its bearing on the welfare of society, the welfare of the public; that is, of the respectable public,—of the respectable public, gentlemen. For in these days, when the spirit of discontent is so wide-spread, all illegal actions have, so to say, a political bearing, my lord, and all illegal actions are wicked, gentlemen of the Jury, since they tend towards the insecurity of society, or in other words, are definitely aimed at the very basis of all morality and religion. Therefore, my lord, I have received instructions from the Home Secretary to prosecute this woman, who, as I shall be able to prove to you, gentlemen of the Jury, by the testimony of three witnesses occupying responsible official positions, has been guilty of a breach at once of the laws of the country and the dictates of morality, and has thereby seriously inconvenienced a very respectable tradesman, nay (*looking at his brief*) three respectable tradesmen. I shall be able to show,

35

gentlemen, that this woman has stolen three loaves of bread: (*impressively*) not one, gentlemen, but three.

A Voice. She's got three children, you palavering black-guard!⁴

[*Confusion.*]

Mr. Justice N. (who has made an elaborate show of composing himself to slumber since the counsel began, here wakes up and cries out) Arrest that man, officer; I will commit him, and give him the heaviest punishment that the law allows of.

[*The* USHER *dives among the audience amidst great confusion, but comes back empty-handed.*

J. N. A most dangerous disturbance! A most dangerous disturbance!

Mr. H. Gentlemen of the Jury, in confirmation of my remarks on the spirit that is abroad, I call your attention to the riot which has just taken place, endangering, I doubt not, the life of his lordship, and your own lives, gentlemen, so valuable to—to—to—in short, to yourselves. Need I point out to you at any length, then, the danger of allowing criminals, offenders against the sacred rights of property, to go at large? This incident speaks for me, and I have now nothing to do but let the witnesses speak for themselves. Gentlemen of the Jury, I do not ask you to convict on insufficient evidence; but I *do* ask you not to be swayed by any false sentiment bearing reference to the so-called smallness of the offence, or the poverty of the offender. The law is made for the poor as well as for the rich, for the rich as well as for the poor. The poor man has no more right to shelter himself behind his poverty, than the rich man behind his riches. In short, gentlemen of the Jury, what I ask you in all confidence to do, is to do justice and fear not.—I call Sergeant Sticktoit.

[SERGEANT STICKTOIT *sworn*.]

Mr. H. Well, sergeant, you saw this woman steal the loaves?

Sticktoit. Yes, sir.

Mr. H. All of them?

St. Yes, all.

Mr. H. From different shops, or from one?

St. From three different shops.

Mr. H. Yes, just so. (*Aside:* Then why the devil did he say from one shop when his evidence was taken before?) (*To* ST.) You were an eye-witness of that? You noticed her take all three loaves?

St. (*Aside:* He wants me to say from three different shops; I'm sure I don't know why. Anyhow, I'll say it—and swear it.) (*To the Court*) Yes, I was an eye-witness of the deed; (*pompously*) I followed her, and then I took her.

Mr. H. Yes, then you took her. Please tell the Court how.

St. (*Aside:* Let's see, what did we agree was the likeliest way?) (*To Court*) I saw her take the first loaf and hide it in her shawl; and then the second one; and the second one tumbled down into the mud; and she picked it up again and wiped it with her shawl; and then she took the third; and when she tried to put that with the two others they all three tumbled down; and as she stooped down to pick

37

them up it seemed the best time to take her, as the two constables had come up; so I took her.

Mr. H. Yes; you took her.

St. And she cried.

Mr. H. Ah, she cried. Well, sergeant, that will do; you may go. (*Aside:* The sooner he goes the better. Wouldn't I like to have the cross-examining of him if he was called on the other side!) Constable Potlegoff.

[POTLEGOFF *sworn.*]

Mr. H. Well, constable, did you see the woman take the loaves?

Potlegoff. Yes, sir.

Mr. H. How did she take them?

Pot. Off the counter, sir.

Mr. H. Did she go into the shop to take them?

Pot. Yes, sir. (*Aside:* I thought I was to say into three shops.)

Mr. H. One after another?

Pot. Yes, out of one shop one after another. (*Aside:* Now it's right, I hope.)

Mr. H. (*Aside:* Confound him, he's contradicting the other!) (*To* POT.) Yes, just so; one after the other. And did you see the second loaf tumble down?

Pot. Yes, sir.

Mr. H. When was that?

Pot. As she took it off the counter.

38

Mr. H. Yes, *after* she took it off the counter, in the street?

Pot. No, sir. (*Catching the* SERGEANT'S *eye.*) I mean yes, sir, and she wiped the mud off them; the sergeant saw her—and I saw her.

A Voice. Off IT, you liar! 'twas the second loaf, the single loaf, the other liar said!

[*Confusion. The* JUDGE *wakes up and splutters, and tries to* say something; *the* USHER *goes through the audience, but finds no one:* HUNGARY *spreads out his hands to the Jury, appealingly.*]

Mr. H. Yes, so it was in the street that you saw the loaves fall down?

Pot. Yes, sir; it was in the street that I saw it tumble down.

A Voice. You mean *them,* you fool! You haven't got the story right yet!

[*Confusion again. The* JUDGE *sits up and stares like a man awaked from a nightmare, then calls out* Officer! Officer! *very loud. The* USHER *goes his errand again, and comes back bootless.*]

Mr. H. (*very blandly*). It was in the street that you saw the three loaves fall down?

Pot. Yes, it was in the street that I saw the loaf fall down.

Mr. H. Yes, in the street; just so, in the street. You may go (*Aside:* for a damned fool!). Constable Strongithoath.

[CONSTABLE STRONGITHOATH *sworn.*]

Mr. H. Constable, did you see this robbery?

Strong. I saw it.

Mr. H. Tell us what you saw.

Strong. (*very slowly and stolidly, and as if repeating a lesson*). I saw her steal them all—all—all from one shop—from three shops—I followed her—I took her. When she took it up—she let it drop—in the shop—and wiped the street mud off it. Then she dropped them all three in the shop—and came out—and I took her—with the help—of the two constables—and she cried.

Mr. H. You may go (*Aside:* for a new-caught joskin and a fool!). I won't ask him any questions.

J. N. (*waking up, and languid*). Do you call any other witnesses, Mr. Hungary?

Mr. H. No, my lord. (*Aside:* Not if I know it, considering the quality of the evidence. Not that it much matters; the Judge is going to get a conviction; the Jury will do as he tells them—always do.) (*To the Court*): My lord and gentlemen of the Jury, that's my case.

J. N. Well, my good woman, what have you to say to this?

Mary Pinch. Say to it! What's the use of *saying* anything to it? I'd *do* to it, if I could.

J. N. Woman! what do you mean? Violence will not do here. Have you witnesses to call?

M. P. Witnesses! how can I call witnesses to swear that I didn't steal the loaves?

J. N. Well, do you wish to question the witnesses? You have a right to.

40

M. P. Much good that would be! Would you listen to me if I did? I didn't steal the loaves; but I wanted them, I can tell you that. But it's all one; you are going to have it so, and I might as well have stolen a diamond necklace for all the justice I shall get here. What's the odds? It's of a piece with the rest of my life for the last three years. My husband was a handsome young countryman once, God help us! He could live on ten shillings a-week before he married me; let alone that he could pick up things here and there. Rabbits and hares some of them, as why should he not? And I could earn a little too; it was not so bad there. And then and for long the place was a pretty place, the little grey cottage among the trees, if the cupboard hadn't been so bare; one can't live on flowers and nightingale's songs. Then the children came brisk, and the wages came slack; and the farmer got the new reaping-machine, and my binding came to an end; and topping turnips for a few days in the foggy November mornings don't bring you in much, even when you haven't just had a baby. And the skim milk was long ago gone, and the leasing, and the sack of tail-wheat, and the cheap cheeses almost for nothing, and the hedge-clippings, and it was just the bare ten shillings a-week. So at last, when we had heard enough of eighteen shillings a-week up in London, and we scarce knew what London meant, though we knew well enough what ten shillings a-week in the country meant, we said we'd go to London and try it there; and it had been a good harvest, quickly saved, which made it bad for us poor folk, as there was the less for us to do; and winter was creeping in on us. So up to London we came; for says Robert: "They'll let us

41

starve here, for aught I can see: they'll do naught for us; let us do something for ourselves." So up we came; and when all's said, we had better have lain down and died in the grey cottage clean and empty. I dream of it yet at whiles: clean, but no longer empty; the crockery on the dresser, the flitch hanging from the rafters, the pot on the fire, the smell of new bread about; and the children fat and ruddy tumbling about in the sun; and my lad coming in at the door stooping his head a little; for our door is low, and he was a tall handsome chap in those days.—But what's the use of talking? I've said enough: I didn't steal the loaves—and if I had a done, where was the harm?[5]

J. N. Enough, woman? Yes, and far more than enough. You are an undefended prisoner. You have not the advantage of counsel, or I would not have allowed you to go on so long. You would have done yourself more good by trying to refute the very serious accusation brought against you, than by rambling into a long statement of your wrongs against society. We all have our troubles to bear, and you must bear your share of them without offending against the laws of your country—the equal laws that are made for rich and poor alike.

A Voice. You can bear *her* troubles well enough, can't you, old fat-guts?

J. N. (scarcely articulate with rage). Officer! officer! arrest that man, or I will arrest you!

[USHER *again makes a vain attempt to get hold of some one.*]

J. N. (puffing and blowing with offended dignity). Woman, woman, have you anything more to say?

M. P. Not a word. Do what you will with me. I don't care.

J. N. (*impressively*). Gentlemen of Jury, simple as this case seems, it is a most important one under the present condition of discontent which afflicts this country, and of which we have had such grievous manifestations in this Court to-day. This is not a common theft, gentlemen—if indeed a theft has been committed—it is a revolutionary theft, based on the claim on the part of those who happen unfortunately to be starving, to help themselves at the expense of their more fortunate, and probably—I may say certainly—more meritorious countrymen. I do not indeed go so far as to say that this woman is in collusion with those ferocious ruffians who have made these sacred precincts of justice ring with their ribald and threatening scoffs. But the persistence of these riotous interruptions, and the ease with which their perpetrators have evaded arrest, have produced a strange impression in my mind. (*Very impressively.*) However, gentlemen, that impression I do not ask you to share; on the contrary, I warn you against it, just as I warn you against being moved by the false sentiment uttered by this woman, tinged as it was by the most revolutionary—nay, the most bloodthirsty feeling. Dismiss all these non-essentials from your minds, gentlemen, and consider the evidence only; and show this mistaken woman the true majesty of English Law by acquitting her—if you are not satisfied with the abundant, clear, and obviously unbiassed evidence, put before you with that terseness and simplicity of diction which distinguishes our noble civil force. The case is so free from intricacy, gentlemen, that I

43

need not call your attention to any of the details of that evidence. You must either accept it as a whole and bring in a verdict of guilty, or your verdict must be one which would be tantamount to accusing the sergeant and constables of wilful and corrupt perjury; and I may add, wanton perjury; as there could be no possible reason for these officers departing from the strict line of truth. Gentlemen, I leave you to your deliberations.

Foreman of Jury. My lord, we have already made up our minds. Your lordship need not leave the Court: we find the woman guilty.

J. N. (*gravely nodding his head*). It now remains for me to give sentence. Prisoner at the bar, you have been convicted by a jury of your countrymen—

A Voice. That's a lie! You convicted her: you were judge and jury both.

J. N. (*in a fury*). Officer, you are a disgrace to your coat! Arrest that man, I say. I would have had the Court cleared long ago, but that I hoped that you would have arrested the ruffian if I gave him a chance of repeating his— his crime.

[*The* USHER *makes his usual promenade.*]

J. N. You have been convicted by a jury of your countrymen of stealing three loaves of bread; and I do not see how in the face of the evidence they could have come to any other verdict. Convicted of such a serious offence, this is not the time and place to reproach you with other misconduct; and yet I could almost regret that it is not possible to put you once more in the dock, and try you for conspir-

44

acy and incitement to riot; as in my own mind I have no doubt that you are in collusion with the ruffianly revolutionists, who, judging from their accent, are foreigners of a low type, and who, while this case has been proceeding, have been stimulating their bloodstained souls to further horrors by the most indecent verbal violence. And I must here take the opportunity of remarking that such occurrences could not now be occurring, but for the ill-judged leniency of even a Tory Government in permitting that pest of society the unrespectable foreigner to congregate in this metropolis.[6]

A Voice. What do they do with you, you blooming old idiot, when you goes abroad and waddles through the Loover?

J. N. Another of them! another of those scarcely articulate foreigners! This is a most dangerous plot! Officer, arrest everybody present except the officials. I will make an example of everybody: I will commit them all.

Mr. H. (leaning over to JUDGE). I don't see how it can be done, my lord. Let it alone: there's a Socialist prisoner coming next; you can make him pay for all.

J. N. Oh! there is, is there? All right—all right. I'll go and get a bit of lunch (*offering to rise*).

Clerk. Beg pardon, my lord, but you haven't sentenced the prisoner.

J. N. Oh, ah! Yes. Oh, eighteen months' hard labour.

M. P. Six months for each loaf that I didn't steal! Well, God help the poor in a free country! Won't you save all further trouble by hanging me, my lord? Or if you won't

45

hang me, at least hang my children: they'll live to be a nuisance to you else.

J. N. Remove the woman. Call the next case. (*Aside:* And look sharp; I want to get away.)

[*Case of* JOHN *or* JACK FREEMAN *called.*]

Mr. H. I am for the prosecution, my lord.

J. N. Is the prisoner defended?

Jack Freeman. Not I.

J. N. Hold your tongue, sir! I did not ask you. Now, brother Hungary.

Mr. H. Once more, my lord and gentlemen of the Jury, I rise to address you; and, gentlemen, I must congratulate you on having the honour of assisting on two State trials on one day; for again I am instructed by the Secretary of State for the Home Department to prosecute the prisoner. He is charged with sedition and incitement to riot and murder, and also with obstructing the Queen's Highway.[7] I shall bring forward overwhelming evidence to prove the latter offence—which is, indeed, the easiest of all offences to be proved, since the wisdom of the law has ordained that it can be committed without obstructing anything or anybody. As for the other, and what we may excusably consider the more serious offence, the evidence will, I feel sure, leave no doubt in your minds concerning the guilt of the prisoner. I must now give you a few facts in explanation of this case. You may not know, gentlemen of the Jury, that in the midst of the profound peace which this glorious empire now enjoys; in spite of the liberty which is the proud possession of every Briton, whatever his rank or fortune; in

spite of the eager competition and steadily and swiftly rising wages for the services of the workmen of all grades, so
that such a thing as want of employment is unheard of
amongst us; in spite of the fact that the sick, the infirm,
the old, the unfortunate, are well clothed and generously
fed and housed in noble buildings, miscalled, I am free to
confess, *work*houses, since the affectionate assiduity of our
noble Poor Law takes every care that if the inmates are of
no use to themselves they shall at least be of no use to any
one else,—in spite of all these and many kindred blessings
of civilisation, there are, as you may not know, a set of
wicked persons in the country, mostly, it is true, belonging
to that class of non-respectable foreigners of whom my
lord spoke with such feeling, taste, and judgment, who are
plotting, rather with insolent effrontery than crawling se-
crecy, to overturn the sacred edifice of property, the foun-
dation of our hearths, our homes, and our altars. Gentlemen
of the Jury, it might be thought that such madmen might
well be left to themselves, that no one would listen to their
ravings, and that the glorious machinery of Justice need no
more be used against them than a crusader's glittering
battle-axe need be brought forward to exterminate the
nocturnal pest of our couches. This indeed has been, I
must say unfortunately, the view taken by our rulers till
quite recently. But times have changed, gentlemen; for
need I tell you, who in your character of shrewd and suc-
cessful men of business understand human nature so well,   *47*
that in this imperfect world we must not reckon on the
wisdom, the good sense of those around us. Therefore you
will scarcely be surprised to hear that these monstrous,
wicked, and disreputable doctrines are becoming popular;

that murder and rapine are eagerly looked forward to under such names as Socialism, revolution, co-operation, profit-sharing, and the like; and that the leaders of the sect are dangerous to the last degree. Such a leader you now see before you. Now I must tell you that these Socialist or Co-operationist incendiaries are banded together into three principal societies,[8] and that the prisoner at the bar belongs to one if not two of these, and is striving, hitherto in vain, for admittance into the third and most dangerous. The Federationist League and the International Federation, to one or both of which this man belongs, are dangerous and malevolent associations; but they do not apply so strict a test of membership as the third body, the Fabian Democratic Parliamentary League, which exacts from every applicant a proof of some special deed of ferocity before admission, the most guilty of their champions veiling their crimes under the specious pretexts of vegetarianism, the scientific investigation of supernatural phenomena, vulgarly called ghost-catching, political economy, and other occult and dull studies.[9] But though not yet admitted a neophyte of this body, the prisoner has taken one necessary step towards initiation, in learning the special language spoken at all the meetings of these incendiaries: for this body differs from the other two in using a sort of cant language or thieves' Latin, so as to prevent their deliberations from becoming known outside their unholy brotherhood. Examples of this will be given you by the witnesses, which I will ask you to note carefully as indications of the dangerous and widespread nature of the conspiracy. I call Constable Potlegoff.

[CONSTABLE POTLEGOFF *sworn*.]

Mr. H. Have you seen the prisoner before?

Pot. Yes.

Mr. H. Where?

Pot. At Beadon Road, Hammersmith.

Mr. H. What was he doing there?

Pot. He was standing on a stool surrounded by a dense crowd.

Mr. H. What else?

Pot. He was speaking to them in a loud tone of voice.

Mr. H. You say it was a dense crowd: how dense? Would it have been easy for any one to pass through the crowd?

Pot. It would have been impossible. I could not have got anywhere near him without using my truncheon—which I have a right to do.

Mr. H. Is Beadon Road a frequented thoroughfare?

Pot. Very much so, especially on a Sunday morning.

Mr. H. Could you hear what he said?

Pot. I could and I did. I made notes of what he said.

Mr. H. Can you repeat anything he said?

Pot. I can. He urged the crowd to disembowel all the inhabitants of London. (*Sensation.*)

49

Mr. H. Can you remember the exact words he used?

Pot. I can. He said, "Those of this capital should have no bowels. You workers must see to having this done."

J. N. Stop a little; it is important that I should get an accurate note of this (*writing*). Those who live in this metropolis must have their bowels drawn out—is that right?

Pot. This capital, he said, my lord.

J. N. (*writing*). This capital. Well, well, well! I cannot guess why the prisoner should be so infuriated against this metropolis. Go on, Mr. Hungary.

Mr. H. (*to witness*). Can you remember any other words he said?

Pot. Yes; later on he said, "I hope to see the last Londoner hung in the guts of the last member of Parliament."

J. N. Londoner, eh?

Pot. Yes, my lord; that is, he meant Londoner.

J. N. You mustn't say what he meant, you must say what you heard him say.

Pot. Capital, my lord.

J. N. I see; (*writing*) The last dweller in the metropolis.

Pot. Capital, my lord.

J. N. Yes, exactly; that's just what I've written—this metropolis.

Pot. He said capital, my lord.

Mr. H. Capital, the witness says, my lord.

J. N. Well, doesn't that mean the same thing? I tell you I've got it down accurately.

J. F. (*who has been looking from one to the other with an amused smile, now says as if he were thinking aloud:*) Well, I *am* damned! what a set of fools!

J. N. What is that you said, sir? Have you no sense of decency, sir? Are you pleading, or are you not pleading? I have a great mind to have you removed.

J. F. (*laughing*). Oh, by all means remove me! I didn't ask to be here. Only look here, I could set you right in three minutes if you only let me.

J. N. Do you want to ask the witness anything? If not, sir hold your tongue, sir. No, sir; don't speak, sir. I can see that you are meditating bullying me; let me advise you, sir, not to try it.

Mr. H. (*to* POT.). Was that the only occasion on which you heard him speaking?

Pot. No; I have heard him speaking in Hyde Park and saying much the same thing, and calling Mr. Justice Nupkins a damned old fool!

J. N. (*writing*). "A damned old fool!" Anything else?

Pot. A blasted old cheat!

J. N. (*writing*). "A blasted old cheat!" (*Cheerfully*) Go on.

Pot. Another time he was talking in a public-house with two men whom I understood to be members of the Fabian League. He was having words with them, and one of them said, "Ah, but you forget the rent of ability"; and he said, "Damn the rent of ability, I will smash their rents of abilities."[10]

Mr. H. Did you know what that meant?

Pot. No; not then.

Mr. H. But you do now?

51

Pot. Yes; for I got into conversation with one of them, who told me that it meant the brain, the skull.

J. N. (writing). "The rent of ability is a cant phrase in use among these people signifying the head."

Mr. H. Well?

Pot. Well, then they laughed and said, "Well, as far as he is concerned, smash it when you can catch it.

Mr. H. Did you gather whose head it was that they were speaking of?

Pot. Yes; his lordship's.

Mr. H. (impressively and plaintively). And *why?*

Pot. Because they said he had jugged their comrades like a damned old smoutch!

J. N. Jugged?

Pot. Put them in prison, my lord.

J. N. (Aside: That Norwich affair.)[11] Wait! I must write my self down a smoutch—smoutch? no doubt a foreign word.

Mr. H. What else have you heard the prisoner say?

Pot. I have heard him threaten to make her Majesty the Queen take in washing.

J. N. Plain washing.

Pot. Yes, my lord.

J. N. Not fancy work?

Pot. No, my lord.

A Juryman. Have you heard him suggest any means of doing all this?

Pot. Yes, sir; for I have attended meetings of his association in disguise, when they were plotting means of exciting the populace.

Mr. H. In which he took part?

Pot. In which he took part.

Mr. H. You heard him arranging with others for a rising of the lower orders?

Pot. Yes, sir; and on the occasion, when I met him in the public-house, I got into conversation with him, and he told me that his society numbered upwards of two millions. (J. F. *grins.*)[12]

The Juryman (*anxiously*). Armed?

Pot. He said there were arms in readiness for them.

Mr. H. Did you find out where?

Pot. Yes; at the premises of the Federationist League, 13 Farringdon Road.

Mr. H. Did you search for them there?

Pot. Yes.

Mr. H. Did you find them?

Pot. No; we found nothing but printing-stock and some very shabby furniture, and the office-boy, and three compositors.

Mr. H. Did you arrest them?

Pot. No; we thought it better not to do so.

Mr. H. Did they oppose your search?

Pot. No.

Mr. H. What did they do?

53

Pot. Well, they took grinders at me and said, "Sold!"

Mr. H. Meaning, doubtless, that they had had an inkling of your search and had sold the arms?

Pot. So we gathered.

J. N. (writing). "They did not find the arms because they had been sold."

Mr. H. Well, Constable, that will do.

J. N. Prisoner, do you wish to ask the Constable any questions?

J. F. Well, I don't know. I strongly suspect that you have made up your mind which way the jury shall make up their minds, so it isn't much use. However, I will ask him three questions. Constable Potlegoff, at how many do you estimate the dense crowd at Beadon Road, when I obstructed?

Pot. Upwards of a thousand.

J. F. H'm; a good meeting! How many were present at that meeting of the Socialist League where we were plotting to make the Queen take in washing?

Pot. Upwards of two hundred.

J. F. Lastly, when I told you in the public-house that we were two millions strong, were you drunk or sober?

Pot. Sober.

J. F. H'm! It's a matter of opinion perhaps as to when a man *is* drunk. Was I sober?

Pot. No; drunk.

J. F. H'm! So I should think. That'll do, Mr. Potlegoff;

I won't muddle your "Rent-of-Ability" any more. Good bye.

[SERGEANT STICKTOIT *called*.]

Mr. H. Have you heard the prisoner speaking?

St. Yes.

Mr. H. Where?

St. At Beadon Road amongst other places: that's where I took him.

Mr. H. What was he doing?

St. Standing on a stool, speaking.

Mr. H. Yes; speaking: to how many people?

St. About a thousand.

Mr. H. Could you get near him?

St. Nowhere near.

Mr. H. Well, can you tell me what he was saying?

St. Well, he said that all the rich people and all the shopkeepers (*glancing at the Jury*) should be disemboweled and flayed alive, and that all arrangements had been made for doing it, if only the workingmen would combine. He then went into details as to where various detachments were to meet in order to take the Bank of England and capture the Queen. He also threatened to smash Mr. Justice Nupkins' "Rent-of-Ability," by which I understood him to mean his skull.

J. N. His—my brains, you mean!

St. No, my lord; for he said that you—that he—hadn't any brains.

55

Mr. H. Did you find any documents or papers on him when he was arrested?

St. Yes; he had a bundle of papers with him.

Mr. H. Like this? (*showing a number of "Commonweal"*)

St. Yes.

J. F. (*Aside:* Two quires that I couldn't sell, damn it!)

Mr. H. We put this paper in, my lord. Your lordship will notice the vileness of the incendiarism contained in it. I specially draw your attention to this article by one Bax,[13] who as you will see, is familiar with the use of dynamite to a fearful extent. (*J. N. reads, muttering "Curse of Civilisation."*) Gentlemen of the Jury that is our case.

J. N. (*looking up from "Commonweal"*). Prisoner at the bar, what have you to say? Do you call witnesses?

J. F. Yes, I call witnesses, but I haven't much to say. I am accused of obstruction, but I shan't argue that point, as I know that I should do myself no good by proving that I had not obstructed. I am accused of being a Socialist and a revolutionist. Well, if you, my lord, and you, gentlemen of the Jury, and the classes to which you belong, knew what Socialism means—and I fear you take some pains not to— you would also know what the condition of things is now, and how necessary revolution is. So if it is a crime to be a Socialist and a revolutionist, I have committed that crime; but the charge against me is that I am a criminal fool, which I am not. And my witnesses will show you, gentlemen of the Jury, that the evidence brought against me is a mass of lies of the silliest concoction. That is, they will show it you if you are sensible men and understand your

56

position as jurymen, which I almost fear you do not. Well, it will not be the first time that the judge has usurped the function of the jury, and I would go to prison cheerfully enough if I could hope it would be the last.

[*He pauses as if to listen. Confused noises and the sound of the "Marseillaise" a long way off.*]

(*Aside:* What is it, I wonder?—No; it's nothing.)

J. N. Prisoner, what is the matter with you? You seem to be intoxicated; and indeed I hope you are, for nothing else could excuse the brutality of your language.

J. F. Oh, don't put yourself out, my lord. You've got the whip-hand of me, you know. I thought I heard an echo; that's all. Well, I will say no more, but call the Archbishop of Canterbury.

[*Enter the* ARCHBISHOP,[14] *who is received with much reverence and attention. He is sworn.*]

J. F. Your Grace, were you present at the meeting at Beadon Road where I was arrested?

Arch. Yes—yes, I was there. Strange to say, it was on a Sunday morning. I needed some little refreshment from the toils of ecclesiastical office. So I took a cab, I admit under the pretext of paying a visit to my brother of London; and having heard the fame of these Socialist meetings, I betook me to one of them for my instruction and profit: for I hold that in these days even those that are highest in the Church should interest themselves in social matters.

57

J. F. Well, my lord, were you pleased with what you saw and heard?

Arch. I confess, sir, that I was disappointed.

J. F. Why, my lord?

Arch. Because of the extreme paucity of the audience.

J. F. Were there a thousand persons present?

Arch. (*severely*). I must ask you not to jest with me in the sacredly respectable precincts of a Court of Justice. To the best of my remembrance, there were present at the commencement of your discourse but three persons exclusive of yourself. That fact is impressed on my mind from the rude and coarse words which you said when you mounted your stool or rostrum to the friend who accompanied you and had under his arm a bundle of a very reprehensible and ribald print called the *Commonweal,* one of which he, I may say, forced me to purchase.

J. F. Well, what did I say?

Arch. You said, "I say, Bill! damned hard lines to have to speak to a lamp-post, a kid, and an old buffer"—by the latter vulgarity indicating myself, as I understand.

J. F. Yes, my lord, so it is. Now let me ask you, if that matters, is Beadon Road a thronged thoroughfare?

Arch. On the contrary; at least on the morning on which I was there, there was a kind of Sabbath rest about it, scarcely broken by the harangue of yourself, sir.

J. F. You heard what I said, my lord?

58

Arch. I did, and was much shocked at it.

J. F. Well, did I say anything about bowels?

Arch. I regret to say that you did.

J. F. Do you remember the words I used?

Arch. Only too well. You said, but at great length and with much embroidery of language more than questionable, that capital had no bowels for the worker, nor owners of capital either; and that since no one else would be kind to them, the workers must be kind to themselves and take the matter into their own hands.

J. N. (*making notes*). Owners of *the capital;* workman must take the matter—take the matter—into their own hands.

J. F. Well, I have no more questions to ask your Grace.

Mr. H. With many excuses, your Grace, *I* will ask you a question.

Arch. Certainly, Mr. Hungary.

Mr. H. You say that the audience was very small; that was at first; but did it not increase as time went on?

Arch. Yes; an itinerant vendor of ices drew up his stall there, and two policemen—these gentlemen—strolled in, and some ten or more others stood round us before the orator had finished.

Mr. H. (*Aside:* H'm! old beggar will be so very specific. Let's try him as to the sedition.) (*To* ARCH.) My lord, you said that you were shocked at what the prisoner said: what was the nature of his discourse?

Arch. I regret to have to say that it was a mass of the most frightful incendiarism, delivered with an occasional air of jocularity and dry humour that made my flesh creep. Amidst the persistent attacks on property he did not spare other sacred things. He even made an attack on my position, stating (wrongly) the amount of my moderate sti-

59

pend.[15] Indeed, I think he recognised me, although I was partially disguised.

J. F. (*Aside:* True for you, old Benson, or else how could I have subpoenaed you?)

Mr. H. I thank your Grace: that will do.

J. F. I now call Lord Tennyson.

[LORD TENNYSON *sworn.*]

J. F. My lord, have you been present, in disguise, at a meeting of the Socialist League in 13 Farringdon Road?

Lord T. What's that to you? What do you want to know for? Yes, I have, if it comes to that.

J. F. Who brought you there?

Lord T. A policeman: one Potlegoff. I thought he was a Russian by his name, but it seems he is an Englishman— and a liar. He said it would be exciting: so I went.

J. F. And was it exciting?

Lord T. NO: it was *dull.*

J. F. How many were present?

Lord T. Seventeen: I counted them, because I hadn't got anything else to do.[16]

J. F. Did they plot anything dreadful?

Lord T. Not that I could hear. They sat and smoked; and one fool was in the chair, and another fool read letters; and then they worried till I was sick of it as to where such and such fools should go to spout folly the next week; and now and then an old bald-headed fool and a stumpy little fool in blue[17] made jokes, at which they laughed a good deal; but I couldn't understand the jokes—and I came away.

J. F. Thank you, my lord.

Mr. H. My lord Tennyson, I wish to ask you a question. You say that you couldn't understand their jokes: but could you understand them when they were in earnest?

Lord T. No, I couldn't: I can't say I tried. I don't want to understand Socialism: it doesn't belong to my time.

[*Exit.*]

J. F. I call Professor Tyndall.[18]

[PROFESSOR TYNDALL *sworn.*]

J. F. Professor Tyndall, have you seen me before?

Pro. T. Yes; I have seen you in a public-house, where I went to collect the opinions of the lower orders against Mr. Gladstone.[19a]

J. F. Who was I with?

Pro. T. You were with a man whom I was told was a policeman in plain clothes, and with some others that I assume to have been friends of yours, as you winked at them and you and they were laughing together as you talked to the policeman.

J. F. Do you see the policeman in Court?

Pro. T. Yes; there he is.

J. F. Was he drunk or sober?

Pro. T. What, now?

J. F. No—then.

Pro. T. (*with decision*). Drunk.

J. F. Was I drunk?

Pro. T. What, now?

J. F. No—then; though you may tell me whether I'm drunk or not now, if you like, and define drunkenness scientifically.

Pro. T. Well, you were so, so.

J. F. Thank you, Professor.

Mr. H. One question, Professor Tyndall. Did you hear what the prisoner was saying to the policeman—who, by the way, was, I suspect, only shamming drunkenness?

J. F. (*Aside:* He could carry a good deal, then.)

Pro. T. Yes. I heard him. He was boasting of the extent and power of the Socialist organisation.

Mr. H. And did you believe it? did it surprise you?

Pro. T. It did not in the least surprise me: it seemed to me the natural consequences of Gladstone's Home Rule Bill.[19b] As to believing it, I knew he was jesting; but I thought that his jesting concealed very serious earnest. He seemed to me a determined, cunning, and most dangerous person.

Mr. H. I thank you, professor.

[*Exit* PRO. T.]

J. N. Prisoner, do you want to re-examine the witnesses? What's that noise outside? They ought to be arrested.

[*"Marseillaise" again without, and tumult nearer.* FREEMAN *listens intently, without heeding the* JUDGE.]

62

J. N. Prisoner, why don't you answer? Your insolence won't serve you here, I can tell you.

J. F. I was listening, Judge; I thought I heard that echo again.

J. N. Echo again! What does the fellow mean? It's my belief you're drunk, sir: that you have stimulated your courage by liquor.

A Voice. Look out for *your* courage, old cockywax; you may have something to try it presently!

J. N. Officer, arrest that pernicious foreigner.

[USHER *promenades once more.*]

J. N. (*Aside:* I don't like it: I'm afraid there is something going to happen.) (*To Court*) Mr. Hungary.

Mr. H. My lord and gentlemen of the Jury, the prisoner's mingled levity and bitterness leaves me little to answer to. I can only say, gentlemen of the Jury, that I am convinced that you will do your duty. As to the evidence, I need make no lengthened comments on it, because I am sure his lordship will save me the trouble. (*Aside:* Trust him!) It is his habit—his laudable habit—to lead juries through the intricacies which beset unprofessional minds in dealing with evidence. For the rest, there is little need to point out the weight of the irrefragable testimony of the sergeant and constable,—men trained to bring forward those portions of the facts which come under their notice which *are* weighty. I will not insult you, my lord, by pointing out to intelligent gentlemen in your presence how the evidence of the distinguished and illustrious personages so vexatiously called by the prisoner, so far from shaking the official evidence, really confirms it. (*Aside:* I wonder what all that row is about? I wish I were out of this and at home.) Gentlemen of the Jury, I repeat that I expect you to do your duty and defend yourselves from the bloodthirsty designs of the dangerous revolutionist now before you.

63

(*Aside:* Well, now I'm off, and the sooner the better; there's a row on somewhere.)

[*Exit.*]

J. N. Gentlemen of the Jury, I need not expatiate to you on the importance of the case before you. There are two charges brought against the prisoner, but one so transcends the other in importance—nay, I may say swallows it up—that I imagine your attention will be almost wholly fixed on that—the charge of conspiring and inciting to riot. Besides, on the lesser charge the evidence is so simple and crystal-clear that I need but allude to it. I will only remark on the law of the case, that committing an obstruction is a peculiar offence, since it is committed by everyone who, being in a public thoroughfare, does not walk briskly through the streets from his starting-place to his goal. There is no need to show that some other person is hindered by him in his loitering, since obviously that *might* be the case; and besides, his loitering might hinder another from forming in his mind a legitimate wish to be there, and so might do him a very special and peculiar injury. In fact, gentlemen, it has been doubted whether this grave offence of obstruction is not always being committed by everybody, as a corollary to the well-known axiom in physics that two bodies cannot occupy the same space at one and the same time. So much, gentlemen, for the lesser accusation. As to the far more serious one, I scarcely know in what words to impress upon you the gravity of the accusation. The crime is an attack on the public safety, gentlemen; if it has been committed, gentlemen—if it has been committed. On that point you are bound by your oaths to decide according to the evidence; and I must tell you that the learned counsel

64

was in error when he told you that I should direct your views as to that evidence. It is for you to say whether you believe that the witnesses were speaking what was consonant with truth. But I am bound to point out to you that whereas the evidence for the prosecution was clear, definite, and consecutive, that for the defence had no such pretensions. Indeed, gentlemen, I am at a loss to discover why the prisoner put those illustrious and respectable personages to so much trouble and inconvenience merely to confirm in a remarkable way the evidence of the sergeant and the constable. His Grace the Archbishop said that there were but three persons present when the prisoner *began* speaking; but he has told us very clearly that before the end of the discourse there were ten, or more. You must look at those latter words, *or more,* as a key to reconcile the apparent discrepancy between his Grace's evidence and that of constable Potlegoff. This, however, is a matter of little importance, after what I have told you about the law in the case of obstruction. His Grace's clear remembrance of the horrible language of the prisoner, and the shuddering disgust that it produced on him, is a very different matter. Although his remembrance of the *ipsissima verba* does not quite tally with that of the constable, it is clear that both the Archbishop and the policeman have noted the real significance of what was said: The owners of this capital, said the prisoner—

J. F. I said nothing of the kind.

J. N. Yes you did, sir. Those were the very words you said: I have got it down in my notes of his Grace's evidence. What is the use of your denying it, when your own witness gives evidence of it? Hold your tongue sir.—And the work-

ing-men, says the prisoner, must take the matter into their
own hands. Take it into *their own hands,* gentlemen, and take
the matter into their hands. What matter are they to take into
their hands? Are we justified in thinking that the prisoner
was speaking metaphorically? Gentlemen, I must tell you
that the maxim that in weighing evidence you need not go
beyond the most direct explanation guides us here; forbids
us to think that the prisoner was speaking metaphorically,
and compels us to suppose that the *matter* which is to be in
the *hands* of the workmen, their very *hands,* gentlemen, is—
what? Why, (*in an awe-struck whisper*) the bowels of the owners of the capital, that is of this metropolis—London! Nor,
gentlemen, are the means whereby those respectable persons, the owners of house property in London, to be dis-
embowelled left doubtful: the raising of armed men by the
million, concealed weapons, and an organisation capable of
frustrating the search for them. Nay, an article in the paper
which impudently calls itself (*reading the "Commonweal"*)
the official journal of the Socialist League, written by one
Bax, who ought to be standing in the same dock with the
prisoner—an article in which he attacks the sacredness of
civilisation—is murky with the word dynamic or dynamite.
And you must not forget, gentlemen, that the prisoner ac-
cepts his responsibility for all these words and deeds. With
the utmost effrontery having pleaded "Not Guilty," he
says, "I am a Socialist and a Revolutionist"!—Thus much,
gentlemen, my duty compels me to lay before you as to the
legal character of the evidence. But you must clearly understand that it rests with you and not with me to decide as
to whether the evidence shows this man to be guilty. It is
you, gentlemen of the Jury, who are responsible for the

verdict, whatever it may be; and I must be permitted to add that letting this man loose upon society will be a very heavy responsibility for you to accept.

[*The Jury consult: the noise outside increases.*]

J. F. (*Aside:* Hilloa! what *is* going on? I begin to think there's a row up!)

Foreman of the Jury. My lord, we are agreed upon our verdict.

J. N. Do you find the prisoner at the bar "Guilty" or "Not Guilty"?

F. of J. Guilty, my lord.

J. F. Just *so*.

J. N. Prisoner at the bar, you have been fairly tried and found guilty by a jury of your fellow-countrymen of two most serious offences—crimes, I should say. If I had not to pronounce sentence upon one whose conscience is seared and case-hardened to an unexampled degree, I might have some words to say to you. (*Aside:* And also if I didn't want to get out of this as quick as I can; for I'm sure there is some row going on.) As it is, I will add no words to my sentence. (*Aside:* I wish I were off, but let's give it him hot and heavy!) I sentence you to six years' penal servitude and to pay a fine of £100.

J. F. Well, its pretty much what I expected of *you*. As to the £100, don't you wish you may get it; and as to the six years—

[*Great noise; "Marseillaise" sung quite close; hammering on the doors.*]

J. F. Hark! what's that?

67

J. N. (in a quavering voice). Remove the prisoner!

[*Enter a* SOCIALIST ENSIGN *with a red flag in his hand.*]

S. E. Remove the prisoner! Yes, that's just what I've come to do, my lord. The Tables are Turned now!

J. N. (rising and prepared to go). Arrest that man!

S. E. Yes, do—if you can.

J. F. What does it all mean, Bill?

S. E. The very beginning of it, Jack. It seems we have not been sanguine enough. The Revolution we were all looking forward to had been going on all along, and now the last act has begun. The reactionists are fighting, and pretty badly too, for the soldiers are beginning to remember that they too belong to the "lower classes"—the lower classes—hurrah! You must come along at once, Freeman; we shall want you in our quarter. Don't waste another minute with these fools.

J. N. (screaming). Help, help! Murder, murder!

S. E. Murder!—murder a louse! Who's hurting you, old gentleman? Don't make such a noise. We'll try and make some use of you when we have time, but we must bustle now. Come on, Jack. Stop a bit, though; where's the Clerk of the Court? Oh, there! Clerk, we shall want this Court-house[20] almost directly to use for a free market for this district. There have been too many people starving and half-starving this long time; and the first thing that we've got to see to is that every one has enough to eat, drink, and wear, and a proper roof over his head.

J. N. Murder! thieves! fire!

S. E. There, there! Don't make such a row, old fellow! Get out of this, and bellow in the fields with the horned cattle, if you must bellow. Perhaps they'll want Courts of Justice now, as we don't. And as for you, good fellows, all give a cheer for the Social Revolution which has Turned the Tables; and so—to work—to work!

[JUDGE *screams and faints, and Curtain falls.*]

PART II.

SCENE.—*The Fields near a Country Village; a Copse close by.*

Time—After the Revolution.

[*Enter* CITIZEN (*late* JUSTICE) NUPKINS. *He looks cautiously about to right and left, then sits down on the ground.*]

C. N. Now I think I may safely take a little rest; all is quiet here. Yet there are houses in the distance, and wherever there are houses now, there are enemies of law and order. Well, at least, here is a good thick copse for me to hide in in case anybody comes. What am I to do? I shall be hunted down at last. It's true that those last people gave me a good belly-full, and asked me no questions; but they looked at me very hard. One of these times they will bring me before a magistrate, and then it will be all over with me. I shall be charged as a rogue and a vagabond, and made to give an account of myself; and then they will find out who I am, and then I shall be hanged—I shall be hanged— I, Justice Nupkins! Ah, the happy days when *I* used to sentence people to be hanged! How easy life was then, and now how hard!

71

[*Hides his face in his hands and weeps.*]

[*Enter* MARY PINCH, *prettily dressed.*]

M. P. How pleasant it is this morning! These hot late summer mornings, when the first pears are ripening, and the wheat is nearly ready for cutting, and the river is low and weedy, remind me most of the times when I was a little freckle-faced child, when I was happy in spite of everything, though it was hard lines enough sometimes. Well, well, I can think of those times with pleasure now; it's like living the best of the early days over again, now we are so happy, and the children like to grow up straight and comely, and not having their poor little faces all creased into anxious lines. Yes, I am my old self come to life again; it's all like a pretty picture of the past days. They were brave men and good fellows who helped to bring it about: I feel almost like saying my prayers to them. And yet there were people—yes, and poor people too—who couldn't bear the idea of it. I wonder what they think of it now. I wish, sometimes, I could make people understand how I felt when they came to me in prison, where all things were so miserable that, heaven be praised! I can't remember its misery now, and they brought Robert to me, and he hugged me and kissed me, and said, when he stood away from me a little, "Come, Mary, we are going home, and we're going to be happy; for the rich people are gone, and there's no more starving or stealing." And I didn't know what he meant, but I saw such a look in his eyes and in the eyes of those who were with him, that my feet seemed scarcely on the ground; as if I were going to fly. And how tired out I was with happiness before the day was done! Just to think that

72

my last-born child will not know what to be poor meant; and nobody will ever be able to make him understand it. [NUPKINS *groans.*] Hilloa! What's the matter? Why, there's a man ill or in trouble; an oldish man, too. Poor old fellow! Citizen, what's the matter? How can I help you?

C. N. (*jumping up with a howl*). Ah, they are upon me! That dreadful word "citizen"! (*Looks at M. P. and staggers back*). Oh, Lord! is it? Yes, it *is*—the woman that I sentenced on that horrible morning, the last morning I adorned the judicial bench.

M. P. What *is* the matter? And how badly you're dressed; and you seem afraid. What *can* you be afraid of? If I am not afraid of the cows, I am sure you needn't be—with your great thick stick, too. (*She looks at him and laughs, and says aside,* Why to be sure, if it isn't that silly, spiteful old man that sentenced me on the last of the bad days before we all got so happy together!) (*To* N.) Why, Mr. Nupkins—citizen—I remember you; you are an old acquaintance: I'll go and call my husband.

C. N. Oh, no! no! don't! *please* don't!—(*Aside:* There, there, I'm done for—can I run away?—No use—perhaps I might soften her. I used to be called eloquent—by the penny-a-liners. I've made a jury cry—I think—let me try it. Gentlemen of the Jury, remember the sad change in my client's position! remember.—Oh, I'm going mad, I think— she remembers me) (*Kneels before her*) Oh, woman, woman, spare me! Let me crawl into the copse and die quietly there!

M. P. Spare you, citizen? Well, I could have spared you once, well enough, and so could many another poor devil

73

have done. But as to dying in the copse, no, I really can't let you do that. You must come home to our house, and we'll see what can be done with you. It's our old house, but really nice enough, now; all that pretty picture of plenty that I told you about on that day when you were so hard upon me has come to pass, and more.

C. N. Oh, no! I can't come!

M. P. Oh, yes; you can get as far as that, and we'll give you something to eat and drink, and then you'll be stronger. It will really please me, if you'll come; I'm like a child with a new toy, these days, and want to show new-comers all that's going on. Come along, and I'll show you the pretty new hall they are building for our parish; it's such a pleasure to stand and watch the lads at work there, as merry as grigs. Hark! you may hear their trowels clinking from here. And, Mr. Nupkins, you mustn't think I stole those loaves; I really didn't.

C. N. Oh, dear me! Oh, dear me! She wants to get me away and murder me! I won't go.

M. P. How *can* you talk such nonsense? Why, on earth, should I murder you?

C. N. (*sobbing*). Judicially, judicially!

M. P. How silly you are! I really don't know what you mean. Well, if you won't come with me, I'm off; but you know where to go when you want your dinner. But if you still owe me a grudge, which would be very silly of you, any of the people in the houses yonder will give you your food.

74

[*Exit.*]

C. N. There! She's going to fetch some ferocious revolutionaries to make an end of me. It's no use trying to stop her now. I will flee in another direction; perhaps I shan't always meet people I've sentenced.

[*As he is going he runs up against* WILLIAM JOYCE, *once* SOCIALIST ENSIGN, *entering from the other side.*]

William Joyce. Hilloa, citizen! look out! (*looking at him*) But I say, what's the matter with you? You are queerly rigged. Why, I haven't seen a man in such a condition for many a long day. You're like an ancient ruin, a dream of past times. No, really I don't mean to hurt your feelings. Can I do anything to help you?

[*C. N. covers his face with his hands and moans.*]

W. J. Hilloa! Why, I'm blessed if it isn't the old bird who was on the bench that morning, sentencing comrade Jack! What's *he* been doing, I wonder? I say, don't you remember me, citizen? I'm the character who came in with the red flag that morning when you were playing the last of your queer games up yonder. Cheer up, man! we'll find something for you to do, though you have been so badly educated.

C. N. Spare me, I entreat you! Don't let it be known who I am, pray don't, or I shall certainly be hanged. Don't hang me; give me hard labour for life, but don't hang me! Yes, I confess I was Judge Nupkins; but don't give me up! I'll be your servant, your slave all my life; only don't bring me before a magistrate. They are so unfair, and so hard!

W. J. Well, what do you think of a judge, old fellow?

C. N. That's nearly as bad, but not quite; because sometimes there's a cantankerous blackguard on the jury who won't convict, and insists on letting a man off. But, please, pray think better of it, and let it be a private matter, if you must needs punish me. I won't bring an action against you, whatever you do. Don't make it a judicial matter! Look here, I'll sign a bond to be your servant for ever without wages if you will but feed me. I suffer so from not having my meals regularly. If you only knew how bad it is to be hungry and not to be sure of getting a meal.

W. J. Yes, Nupkins; but you see, I *do* know only too well—but that's all gone by. Yet, if you had only known that some time ago, or let's say, guessed at it, it might have been the better for you now.

C. N. (*Aside:* Oh, how jeering and hard he looks!) Oh, spare me, and don't send me to the workhouse! You've no idea how they bully people there. I didn't mean to be a bad or hard man; I didn't indeed.

W. J. Well, I must say if you meant to be anything else, you botched the job! But I suppose, in fact, you didn't mean anything at all.—So much the worse for you. (*Aside:* I must do a little cat and mouse with him).

C. N. Oh, spare me, spare me! I'll work so hard for you. Keep it dark as to who I am. It will be such an advantage you're having me all to yourself.

W. J. Would it, indeed? Well, I doubt that.

C. N. Oh, I think so. I really am a good lawyer.

W. J. H'm, that would be rather less useful than a dead jackass—unless one came to the conclusion of making cat's meat of you.

C. N. (*aside,* Oh, I'm sick at heart at his hinted threats). Mr. Socialist, don't you see I could put you up to all sorts of dodges by which you could get hold of odds and ends of property—as I suppose you have some sort of property still—and the titles of the land must be very shaky just after a revolution? I tell you I could put you up to things which would make you a person of great importance; as good as what a lord used to be.

W. J. (*aside,* Oh, you old blackguard! What's bred in the bone won't come out of the flesh. I really must frighten the old coward a little; besides, the council *has* got to settle what's to be done with him, or the old idiot will put us to shame by dying on our hands of fright and stupidity.) (*To* N.) Nupkins, I really don't know what to do with you as a slave; I'm afraid that you would corrupt the morals of my children; that you would set them quarrelling and tell them lies. There's nothing for it but you must come before the Council of our Commune:[21] they'll meet presently under yonder tree this fine day.

C. N. No, no, don't! Pray let me go and drag out the remainder of a miserable existence without being brought before a magistrate and sent to prison! You don't know what a dreadful thing it is.

W. J. You're wrong again, Nupkins. I know all about it. The stupid red tape that hinders the Court from getting at the truth; the impossibility of making your stupid judge understand the real state of the case, because he is not thinking of you and your life as a man, but of a set of rules drawn up to allow men to make money of other people's

77

misfortunes; and then to prison with you; and your miserable helplessness in the narrow cell, and the feeling as if you must be stifled; and not even a pencil to write with, or knife to whittle with, or even a pocket to put anything in. I don't say anything about the starvation diet, because other people besides prisoners were starved or half-starved. Oh, Nupkins, Nupkins! it's a pity you couldn't have thought of all this before.

C. N. (*aside:* Oh, what terrible revenge is he devising for me?) (*to* W. J.) Sir, sir, let me slip away before the Court meets. (*Aside:* A pretty Court, out in the open-air! Much they'll know about law!)

W. J. Citizen Nupkins, don't you stir from here! You'll see another old acquaintance presently—Jack Freeman, whom you were sending off to six years of it when the red flag came in that day.—And in good time here he is.

[*Enter* JACK FREEMAN, *sauntering in dressed in a blouse, smoking, a billycock*22 *on his head, and his hands in his pockets.*]

W. J. There's your judge, Citizen Nupkins! No, Jack, you needn't take your hands out of your pockets to shake hands with me; I know your ways and your manners. But look here! (*pointing to* NUPKINS).

J. F. Why, what next? There's no mistaking him, it's my old acquaintance Mr. Justice Nupkins. Why you seem down on your luck, neighbour. What can I do to help you?

78

[NUPKINS *moans.*]

W. J. (*winking at* FREEMAN). You've got to try him, Jack.

J. F. Why, what has he been doing? (*Aside,* I say, old fellow, what game are you up to now?)

W. J. Doing? why nothing. That's just it; something must be done with him. He must come before the council; but I'm afraid he's not of much use to anyone. (*Aside,* I say, Jack, he is a mere jelly of fear: thinks that we are going to kill him and eat him, I believe. I must carry it on a little longer; don't spoil all my fun.)

J. F. (*Aside, to* W. J.) Well, certainly he deserves it, but take care that he doesn't die of fear on your hands, Bill. (*Aloud*) Well, the council will meet in a minute or two, and then we will take his case.

C. N. (*to* J. F.) Oh, sir, sir, spare me and don't judge me! I'll be servant to you all my life!

W. J. Why Nupkins, what's this? You promised to be servant to *me!*

J. F. Citizen Nupkins, I really must say thank-you for nothing. What the deuce could I do with a servant? Now don't you trouble yourself; the council will see to your affairs. And in good time here come the neighbours.

[*Enter the Neighbours,* ROBERT PINCH, MARY PINCH, *and others.*]

W. J. Now for it, Nupkins! Bear your own troubles as well as you used to bear other peoples', and then you'll do very well.

JACK FREEMAN *takes his seat on the ground under the tree, the others standing and sitting about him;* WILLIAM JOYCE *makes a shew of guarding* NUPKINS, *at which the neighbours look rather astonished; but he nods and winks to them, and they see there is some joke toward and say nothing.*

J. F. Well, neighbours, what's the business to-day?

1st Neighbour. I have to report that three loads of that oak for the hall-roof have come to hand; it's well-seasoned good timber, so there need be no hitch in the building now.[23]

2nd Neighbour. Well, chairman, we sent off the wool to the north-country communes last week, and they are quite satisfied with it. Their cloth has come to hand rather better than worse than the old sample.

3rd Neighbour. I have to report that the new wheel at the silk mill is going now, and makes a very great improvement. It gives us quite enough power even when the water is small; so we shan't want a steam-engine after all.

J. F. When do we begin wheat harvest?

3rd Neighbour. Next Thursday in the ten-acre; the crop is heavy and the weather looks quite settled; so we shall have a jolly time of it.

J. F. Well, I'm glad I know in good time; for I never like to miss seeing the first row of reapers going into the corn. Is there anything else?

W. J. Well, there's one troublesome business, chairman (*looks at* C. N., *who trembles and moans*) There's that dog we caught, that thief, that useless beast. What is to be done with him?

C. N. (*Aside,* That's me! that's me! To think that a justice should be spoken of in such language! What am I to do? What am I to do?)

2nd Neighbour. Well, chairman, I think we must shoot him. Once a thief always a thief, you see, with that kind of brute. I'm sorry, because he has been so badly brought up;

and though he is an ugly dog, he is big and burly; but I must say that I think it must be done, and as soon as possible. He'll be after the girls if we don't do it at once!

C. N. (*Aside:* What! have they got hold of that story, then?)

J. F. Well, neighbours, what's to be said? anybody against it? Is this unpleasant business agreed to?

All. Agreed, agreed.

J. F. Well, then, let the dog be shot. Bill, it's your turn for an ugly job this time: you must do it.

W. J. Well, if it must be, it must. I'll go and get a gun in a minute.

C. N. Oh, God! to think of their disposing of a fellow-man's life with so little ceremony! And probably they will go and eat their dinners afterwards and think nothing of it. (*Throwing himself on his knees before* JACK FREEMAN.) Oh, your Socialist worship! Oh, citizen my lord! spare me, spare me! Send me to prison, load me with chains, but spare my life!

J. F. Why, what ails the man? Chains! we don't use chains for that sort of thing. They're good to fasten up boats with, and for carts, and such like; so why should we waste them by ornamenting you with them? And as to prison, we can't send you to prison, because we haven't got one. How could we have one? who would be the jailer? No, no; we can't be bothered with you in prison. You must learn to behave decently.

C. N. What! have you no punishment but death, then? O! what am I to do? what am I to do?

1st Neighbour. Do? Why, behave decently.

C. N. But how can I behave decently when I'm dead?
(*Moans.*)

2nd Neighbour. But, neighbour, you must die some time
or another, you know. Make the most of your time while
you are alive.

C. N. Have you the heart to say such things to a man
whom you are going to shoot in a few minutes? How horrible! Oh, look here! if you haven't got a prison, build one
for me! or make one out of a cellar, and lock me up in it;
but don't shoot me—don't!

W. J. Well, old acquaintance, to want a prison all to
your own cheek! This is individualism, with a vengeance! It
beats Auberon Herbert.[24] But who is going to shoot you?

C. N. Why, you. He said shoot the dog (*weeping*).

W. J. Well, citizen, I must say that either your estimate
of yourself is modest, or your conscience is bad, that you
must take that title to yourself! No; it *is* a bad business, but
not so bad as that. It's not you that we're going to shoot,
but a poor devil of a dog—a real dog, with a tail, you
know—who has taken to killing sheep. And I'm sorry to
say that social ethics have given me the job of shooting
him. But come, now, you shall do it for me: you used to be
a great upholder of capital punishment.

82

C. N. But what are you going to do with me, then?
How are you going to punish me?

J. F. Punish you? how can we punish you? who do you
think is going to do such work as that! People punish oth-

ers because they like to: and we don't like to. Once more, learn to live decently.

C. N. But how *am* I to live?

J. F. You must work a little.

C. N. But what at, since you object to lawyers?

J. F. Look round you, friend, at the fields all yellowing for harvest,—we will find you work to do.

C. N. (*Aside:* Ah, I see. This means hard labour for life, after all. Well, I must submit. Unhappy Nupkins! (*To* FREE-MAN) But who is to employ me? You will have to find me a master: and perhaps he won't like to employ me.

J. F. My friend, we no more have masters than we have prisons: the first make the second. You must employ your-self: and you must also employ something else.

C. N. What? I don't understand.

J. F. Mother Earth, and the traditions and devices of all the generations of men whom she has nourished. All that is for you, Nupkins, if you only knew it.

C. N. I still do not comprehend your apologue.

J. F. No? Well, we must put aside abstractions and get to the concrete. What's this, citizen? (*showing a spade.*)

C. N. That is an instrument for effodiation.

J. F. Otherwise called a spade. Well, to use your own jargon, citizen, the sentence of this court is that you do take this instrument of effodiation, commonly called a spade, and that you do effodiate your livelihood therewith; in other words, that you do dig potatoes and other roots and worts during the pleasure of this court. And, to drop jargon, since you are so badly educated our friend Robert Pinch—Mary's husband—will show you how to do it. Is that agreed to, neighbours?

All. Agreed, agreed.

W. J. (*rather surlily*). I don't think he will get on well. Now he knows we are not going to serve him out, he is beginning to look sour on us for being happy. You see, he will be trying some of his old lawyers' tricks again.

J. F. Well, Bill, it won't much matter. He can't hurt us; so we will hope the best for him.

M. P. Should we hurt his feelings by being a little merry in his presence now?

J. F. Well, I think we may risk it. Let those of you who are not too lazy to dance, as I am, do so to the tune that sprang up at the dawn of freedom in the days of our great-grandfathers.

[*They dance round* CITIZEN NUPKINS, *singing the following words to the tune of the "Carmagnole":*][25]

> What's this that the days and the days have done?
> Man's lordship over man hath gone.
>
> How fares it, then, with high and low?
> Equal on earth, they thrive and grow.
>
>> Bright is the sun for everyone;
>> Dance we, dance we the Carmagnole.
>
> How deal ye, then, with pleasure and pain?
> Alike we share and bear the twain.
>
> And what's the craft whereby ye live?
> Earth and man's work to all men give.

How crown ye excellence of worth?
With leave to serve all men on earth.

What gain that lordship's past and done?
World's wealth or all and every one.

[FREEMAN *and* NUPKINS *come to the front.*]

J. F. Well, Nupkins, you see you have got the better of us damned Socialists after all. For in times past you used to bully us and send us to prison and hang us, and we had to put up with it; and now you and yours are no longer masters, there *are* no masters, and there is nobody to bully you. How do you like it, old fellow? (*clapping him on the shoulder.*)

C. N. (*bursting into tears*). A world without lawyers!— oh, dear! oh, dear! To think that I should have to dig potatoes and see everybody happy!

J. F. Well, Nupkins, you must bear it. And for my part, I can't be very sorry that you feel it so keenly. When scoundrels lament that they can no longer be scoundrels for lack of opportunity, it is certain that THE TABLES ARE TURNED.

THE END.

TEXTUAL NOTES

1. *Justice Nupkins*. According to George Bernard Shaw, Morris's depiction of the biased courtroom judge, Nupkins, was modeled after Sir Peter Edlin, well-known in socialist circles for his sentencing of socialists on charges of "obstruction," which "was always proved by getting a policeman to swear that if any passerby or vehicle had wished to pass over the particular spot in a thoroughfare on which the speaker or audience happened to be standing, their presence would have obstructed him" (Weintraub 1969, 153). Shaw noted the absurdity of "sending a man to prison for two months because another man could not walk through him" (Shaw 1932, 2: 153).

2. *La-di-da's sentence*. Nupkins sentences Mr. La-di-da to imprisonment "as a first-class misdemeanant for the space of one calendar month," adding that, to a person of his resources, the sentence "should not be very irksome." Until well into the twentieth century, prisoners from "socially superior" ranks were allowed to make use of their financial resources while in prison, often occupying their own rooms with their own furnishings and hiring servants from among the lower classes of prisoners. It was not until 1947 that the Labour Government in power abolished a prison system or-

ganized into three divisions, the third for "common criminals," a second for "a more deserving class," and the first for intellectuals and members of the upper classes (*New York Law Journal,* 15 October 1990, on LEXIS).

3. *Mr. Hungary.* As the prosecuting attorney in Morris's courtroom farce, Hungary epitomizes Morris's distaste for the legal profession, and by Part II of the play "a good lawyer" is deemed "less useful than a dead jackass." In his lecture, "Useful Work Versus Useless Toil," Morris condemned lawyers as "the parasites of property . . . too often of no use save as supporters of the system of folly, fraud, and tyranny of which they form a part" (Morton 1973, 90).

4. *A Voice.* Morris's friends and comrades in the Nupkins' audience would have recognized the humorous "role" of the voice interrupting Hungary's cross examination of the witnesses against Mary Pinch as a clever allusion to his own role in the trial of the Dod Street affair (20 September 1885), during which Morris was arrested for having called out "Shame" and hissing aloud against the judge in the courtroom (Thompson 1976, 394–397). The Dod Street "affair" had been a peaceful—albeit large—demonstration protesting other recent "obstruction" persecutions (395).

5. *Mary Pinch's "self-defense."* Mary's lengthy romanticizing of country life and "the little grey cottage among the trees" is an appropriate prelude to Morris's later descriptions of glorified country life in the utopian "Nowhere" depicted in his *News from Nowhere* (1890).

6. *foreigners of a low type.* Nupkins's xenophobic condemnation of "that pest of society the unrespectable foreigner" is Morris's clear allusion to a popularly held conspiracy theory

of the 1880s and 1890s. Anarchism, largely supported by Eastern European immigrants, was believed to be an international conspiracy to overthrow governments by means of violence (see Woodcock 1962).

7. *obstructing the Queen's Highway.* Obstruction charges like those leveled in the Dod Street affair were common, and obviously the easiest way to prosecute "street-preaching" socialists.

8. *three principal societies.* Hungary's explanation of the three principal socialist societies in England, the "Federationist League," the "International Federation" and the "Fabian Democratic Parliamentary League" would have been a grand internal joke to members of the Socialist League (S.L.), the Socialist Democratic Federation (S.D.F.), and the Fabians in the play's audience. Although E. P. Thompson argues that until 1886 the clear distinctions between Fabians and other Socialist groups were nominal (Thompson 1976, 332), by 1887 Morris's arguments against Fabianism (and to some extent Social Democracy as led by Hyndman, which Stanley Pierson contends had much in common with Fabian socialism [Pierson 1979, 33]) rested upon its strategies of gradualism and amelioration with existing political parties and administrative agencies. The humorous description of Fabianism's "special language . . . a sort of cant language or thieves' Latin, so as to prevent their deliberations from becoming known outside their holy brotherhood" was Morris's good-natured parody of the movement. Fabianism was of course ironically the least dangerous and conspiratorial of the existing socialist bodies, and its members were predominantly educated and intellectual members of the middle class. The gentle parody seems to have been appreciated by Fabians such as Shaw.

9. *vegetarianism, ghost-catching, and political economy.* These "specious pretexts" were practiced by, respectively, G. B. Shaw, a vegetarian who was never able to convert the beef-eating Morris; Annie Besant, the spiritually inclined intellectual who became a theosophist; and Sidney Webb, the economist and architect of "a new form of Socialist ideology" (see Pierson, 1979, 30–33).

10. *rent of ability.* The clever verbal confusion over the term "rent of ability" proves to be another Morrisian game with the Fabians; this time more specifically with their radical economic theory of rent. The Fabians' departure from basic Marxist economics began with David Ricardo (1772–1823), whose theory of rent was reinterpreted by Shaw and Webb as a more accurate description of social conflict. While Ricardo argued that labor was the only source of value in any economy, the Fabians claimed that rent could include the "surplus values" of capital and even special abilities. If all surplus rents could be taxed, they argued, it was possible to appropriate them through taxation for the benefit of the whole community. The complex ideas involved in the theory of "rents of ability" were beyond even the most devoted socialists—even Morris himself admitted to not having a very good head for economics—or they were for many an incompatible departure from Marxian socialism (see Pierson 1979, 31 and Holroyd 1988, 178–179 for succinct explanations of the theory). Shaw himself later played with the concept in a chapter of his witty book, *The Intelligent Woman's Guide to Socialism and Capitalism* (1928).

11. *Norwich affair.* Nupkins's aside is a reference to the arrest and subsequent sentencing of two Socialist League members in January of 1887. On 14 January Charles Mowbray

and Fred Henderson were arrested after delivering speeches to a crowd of disgruntled, unemployed laborers, who proceeded to smash windows on their way to voicing their grievances in the Guildhall of Norwich. Mowbray received nine months and Henderson three. Morris recorded his angry reaction to this unreasonable sentencing in the Socialist Diary. For this judge, Morris noted great contempt, and he wrote, "the judge's summing up of the case was amusing and instructive, as showing a sort of survival of the old sort of bullying of the Castlereagh time mixed with a grotesque attempt at modernization on philanthropical lines: it put me in a great rage" (Boos 1981, 20).

12. *society numbered . . . two million.* Potlegoff's "memory" of Jack Freeman's boast of almost two million members in "his society" is good cause for Freeman's grin of response in the stage directions. Although some conspiracy theories may have held that socialism was attracting vast numbers of followers, by 1886 membership in both the S.D.F. and the S.L. was estimated at around 2000 (Thompson 1976, 414). Exaggerations about the numbers of "active Socialists" were not made only by the enemies of the movement. Morris was in fact opposed to a strategy of the S.D.F.'s leader, H. M. Hyndman, who (Morris claimed) aimed "to make the movement seem big, to frighten the powers that be with a turnip bogie which perhaps he almost believes himself" (letter to Joynes, Christmas 1884, cited in Boos 1981, 5).

13. *Bax.* The allusion is to Ernest Belfort Bax (1854–1926), an early theorist of Marxism, fellow member of the S.L., and frequent contributor to *Commonweal,* and an essay written for *Commonweal,* "The Curse of Civilisation," which did speak of the "dynamism" of Marxist principles.

14. *Archbishop.* Although the *Pall Mall Gazette* reviewer remarked that Morris's own playing of the role of the Archbishop of Canterbury was free from impersonation of the current Archbishop, Edward White Benson (1829–1896), Morris may have had some cause for parodying a clergyman who paid little attention to secular politics (*Britannica* 1910 :745) and was said to "have a horror of Socialist ideas" (Barrow 1980, 167). Morris also may have had other bones to pick with Benson. Through the ecclesiastical work of Morris & Co., Morris had become familiar with Benson as the Bishop of Truro (1878–1883), where Benson's plans to make "a clean sweep of everything" in constructing a new cathedral led to "a row" with Morris and the Firm (see letter to George Wardle, 5 September 1879 in Kelvin, 1984, 1987, 2: 520–21). Morris's preservation ideals and work with Anti-Scrape (Society for the Protection of Ancient Buildings) are, of course, widely known.

15. *moderate stipend.* A working class distrust of exorbitantly paid bishops was long-standing in England. According to church historian, Owen Chadwick, popular rumors placed stipends of bishops as high as £10,000 annum (Chadwick 1970, 266). In contrast, the average clergyman in 1881 had a nominal annual earning of only £315.37 (Mitchell 1988, 153).

16. *seventeen [persons present at a meeting of the S.L.].* The truth of Tennyson's obervations (and its denial of the prosecution's claims) are corroborated by *Commonweal* accounts of League meetings and by Morris's frequent notation of numbers in the audiences of different meetings in the Socialist Diary. Twenty appears to be an expected or "normal" showing, while forty or fifty is described as "a crowd" (see Boos 1981, 26).

17. *an old bald-headed fool and a stumpy little fool in blue.*
Morris's self-parody here is evident, a reference to his own
portly build and his characteristic attire, the famous blue serge.
We can only assume that the "old bald-headed fool" is a well-
known League member (perhaps Bax?). The humor would
have been appreciated by League members. Morris also revealed an appreciable sense of humor, and a taste for self-
parody, in several of the prose dialogues he wrote for *Commonweal* (see Wiens 1992, 30–36).

18. *Professor Tyndall.* John Tyndall (1820–1893) was a
prominent natural philosopher and scientist and a close friend
and associate of the more prominent T. H. Huxley. Morris
very likely chose to pick on Tyndall because of his opposition
to Gladstone's Irish Home Rule Bill, a cause for which Morris
was an outspoken proponent. Though Tyndall was a liberal in
politics, he split from Gladstone and took an active part in
opposing it (*Britannica* 1910, 27:500).

19a. *Gladstone* and 19b. *Gladstone's Home Rule Bill.* William
Ewart Gladstone was a Liberal statesman and Prime Minister
of England from 1868–74 and again from 1880–85, 1886, and
1892–94. Morris's earliest involvement in politics was as a
Gladstonian Liberal. Gladstone's Home Rule Bill was introduced before Parliament on 8 April 1886. It provided for an
Irish parliament and executive in Dublin with full powers of
legislation except in certain foreign affairs matters. The bill
was defeated on 8 June 1886 (*Britannica,* 1910, 12:71).

20. *Court-house . . to use for a free market.* Morris's opinion of the government and the judicial system is evident in his
satiric portrayal of "a court of justice" in *The Tables Turned.*
He was later to elaborate on these views in his utopian novel,

93

News from Nowhere, in which other government buildings are converted to more practical uses in a world "after the change." In Chapter Seven, the novel's narrator/dreamer, Guest, finds that the Parliament House has been transformed into a Dung Market (May Morris 1910–15, 16:41). In Chapter Eleven, during a later dialogue with an old historian, Guest hears an "enlightened" perspective on the Law Courts of the nineteenth-century. "I think we shall not be far wrong," says Hammond, "if we say that government was the Law Courts, backed up by the executive, which handled the brute force that the deluded people allowed them to use for their own purposes . . the government by Law Courts and police, which was the real government of the nineteenth century, was not a great success even to the people of that day" (May Morris 1910–15, 16:77).

21. *Council of our Commune.* Although Morris uses the post-revolutionary folk moot as the occasion for a humorous reversal of the bourgeois court of Nupkins, it is, nevertheless, an accurate recreation of the kind of vision for decentralized, communal society that Morris painted in his numerous essays for the cause.

22. *billycock.* Jack Freeman's attire reflects the simple, agrarian nature of his new life. The billycock is the round, low-crowned, soft felt hat most often associated with the peasant (or Bohemian art) class (OED).

23. *I have to report . . . .* The snippet of council business being transacted here in Part II of the play is, I would argue, another example of Morris's effective "imaginative expansion" (or literary representation) of the concept of communal, agrarian and "guild" organization which Michael Holzman identifies in Morris's works of eristic prose between 1883 and 1896 (see Holzman 1990 and Wiens 1992).

24. *Auberon Herbert.* The reference is to the liberal philosopher-politician, Auberon Herbert (1838–1906), who moved through a series of political ideologies before becoming a disciple of Herbert Spencer and his theories of individualism versus the state. Herbert's political ideas, like Spencer's, were incompatible with Morris's envisionment of the individual within community, and Morris addressed his opposition to Spencer's "The Coming Slavery" in an article published in *Justice,* 26 April 1884 (see Kelvin 1984 and 1987, 2: 290n, 328n).

25. *the tune of the "Carmagnole."* The "Carmagnole," a lively song and street dance popular during the French Revolution, was obviously more appropriate to the comedic vein of *The Tables Turned* than would have been the more serious "Internationale," another French tune, but one more often used as an inspirational hymn at socialist meetings and gatherings.

REFERENCES

Arnot, R. Page. 1964. *William Morris: The Man and the Myth.* New York: Monthly Review Press.

Barreca, Regina. 1988. "Introduction." *Last Laughs: Perspectives on Women and Comedy.* New York: Gordon and Breach.

Barrow, Andrew. 1980. *The Flesh is Weak: An Intimate History of the Church of England.* London: H. Hamilton.

Bloomfield, Paul. 1934 (1969). *William Morris.* Folcroft, PA: Folcroft Press.

Boos, Florence, ed. 1981. *William Morris's Socialist Diary.* Iowa City: Windhover Press; London: William Morris Society.

Chadwick, Owen. 1970. *The Victorian Church.* vol. 8. London: Adam and Charles Black.

Crane, Walter. 1907. *An Artist's Reminiscences.* New York: Macmillan.

Grimsted, David. 1968. *Melodrama Unveiled.* Chicago: University of Chicago Press.

Holroyd, Michael. 1988. *Bernard Shaw: The Search for Love.* vol. 1. New York: Random House.

Holzman, Michael. 1990. "The Encouragement and the Warn-

ing of History: William Morris's *A Dream of John Ball.*''
Socialism and the Literary Artistry of William Morris. eds.
Florence Boos and Carole Silver. Columbia, Missouri:
University of Missouri Press.

Kelly, John, ed. 1986. *The Collected Letters of W. B. Yeats,* vol.
1. Oxford: Clarendon.

Kelvin, Norman, ed. 1984, 1987. *The Collected Letters of William Morris.* 3 vols. Princeton, NJ: Princeton University
Press.

Lindsay, Jack. 1975. *William Morris: His Life and Work.* London: Constable.

Mackail, J. W. 1899. *The Life of William Morris.* 2 vols. London:
Longmans, Green and Co.

Mitchell, B. R. 1988. *British Historical Statistics.* Cambridge:
Cambridge University Press.

Morris, May, ed. 1910–15. *The Collected Works of William Morris.*
24 vols. London: Longmans, Green.

————. 1936, 1966. *William Morris: Artist, Writer, Socialist.* 2
vols. Oxford: Oxford University Press.

Morris, William and Belfort Bax. 1893. *Socialism: Its Growth
and Outcome.* London: Swan Sonneuschein and Co.

Morton, A. L. 1973. *The Political Writings of William Morris.*
New York: International Publishers.

Pierson, Stanley. 1973. *British Socialism: The Journey from Fantasy
to Politics.* Cambridge: Harvard University Press.

Rhys, Ernest. 1931. *Everyman Remembers.* New York: Cosmopolitan Book Corporation.

Samuel, Raphael, Ewan MacColl, and Stuart Cosgrove. 1985.
Theatres of the Left: 1880–1935. Boston: Routledge and
Kegan Paul.

Sargent, Lyman Tower. 1990. "William Morris and the Anarchist Tradition." *Socialism and the Literary Artistry of William Morris.* eds. Florence S. Boos and Carole G. Silver. Columbia, Mo.: Univ. of Missouri Press.

Shaw, George Bernard. 1928. *The Intelligent Woman's Guide to Socialism and Capitalism.* New York: Brentanos.

————. 1932. "William Morris as Actor and Dramatist." *Our Theatres in the Nineties,* 2: 212–213.

Stetz, Margaret. "Turning the Tables on Anarchism: Morris and Fin-De-Siecle Comedy." Paper presented for panel of The William Morris Society, MLA, Chicago, Illinois, December 1990.

Thompson, E. P. 1976. *William Morris: Romantic to Revolutionary.* New York: Pantheon Books.

Weintraub, Stanley, ed. 1969. *Shaw: An Autobiography (Selections from his Writings).* New York: Weybright and Talley.

Wiens, Pamela Bracken. "The Reviews are In: Reclaiming the Success of Morris's Socialist Interlude." *Journal of the William Morris Society.* (Spring 1991): 16–21.

————. " 'To See Bigly and Kindly': Dialogue and Dialectic in the Political Discourse of William Morris." *Journal of Pre-Raphaelite Studies* (Fall 1992): 30–36.

Woodcock, George. 1962. *Anarchism: A History of Libertarian Ideas and Movements.* Harmondsworth, Middlesex: Penguin Books.

A NOTE ABOUT THE EDITOR

Pamela Bracken Wiens is an active member of the William Morris Society in the United States, and has contributed articles on Morris to the United States *Newsletter,* the British *Journal of the William Morris Society,* and the *Journal of Pre-Raphaelite Studies.*

THE WILLIAM MORRIS SOCIETY

The William Morris Society, founded in London in 1956, seeks to make the life, works, and ideas of William Morris better known. In recent years, particularly in the United States, the Society's concerns have expanded to cover Morris's friends and followers, especially the Pre-Raphaelite writers and artists and participants in the Aesthetic and Arts and Crafts movements. The Society owns Kelmscott House, Morris's London residence. Its activities (in Britain and the United States) include talks, museum visits, social gatherings, and participation in the annual convention of the Modern Language Association. Members receive quarterly *Newsletters* and the semi-annual *Journal*. For further information contact: The William Morris Society, Kelmscott House, 26 Upper Mall, Hammersmith, London W6 9TA England.